1

MAN AND HIS NATURE TODAY (2012)

(An eccentric look at few issues)

Enyi L. Nwankwo

ISBN: 978-978-51324-4-1

First Published 2013

Published by: AMAC TECHNOLOGIES LTD

CRYSTAL ESTATE, AMUWO-ODUFIN

LAGOS NIGERIA

Tel: +234-803-473-5188, +234-803-305-1446

Email: amactechnologieslimited@gmail.com

DEDICATION

First and most importantly to: Lord GOD Almighty, for awesome grace, favours and a lot more.

Then, some to my bosom friend (who took a relationship stand about 3months before I was born and kept it until about 9.30pm on 22nd August 2011), FI; we give GOD Almighty, all glory for you and much more.

ACKNOWLEDGEMENT

As one, whose education enabled a basic exposure to genetics, I give my parents special thanks for my upbringing and the peculiar inherited streak of work attitude, humour, determination and even quiet stubbornness.

It is obvious to me that I am blessed with not only loved ones who encourage you but also at remarkably quiet times seriously urge you to 'keep-at-it' to complete any pending worthy undertaking. Their list (for this book) is actually a little longer but MC, Zyka, Kay and Uchechi are singled-out:

......talk of a fifth book looking at man, with reference to his environment; I guess, is to show the relevance of some issues many over-look. *-Zyka Nov. 2012.*

......this one, now on human and weather trends; I hope it would be crisp for also the benefit of 'our' group of non-marathon readers?

-Kay Dec. 2012.

......your talk on those disaster patterns are not easy to comprehend; while the Arab Spring issues are worth many learning from.

-MC Jan. 2013.

Charyo fits into a distinct niche; 'quiet and persistent pressure group', almost on daily basis, asking for progress update and when she can start vetting the draft. She eventually, surely did.

To many others, not mentioned: no less regards, thank you and God bless.

Enyi L Nwankwo.(April 2013)

PREFACE

For a writer (who lacks social science training) explanatory remarks for a book that is on some issues of man and his nature today; would much reflect his environmental (ecological) background. As such, an eccentric presentation may not be strange.

Man has long been established (scientifically, religiously etc), as being superior to all other living things. His comparatively much larger brain capacity testifies to that natural endowment. His intelligence scope as such (unlike the animals) includes a general capacity to profit from past experiences, among others. While surely, there is a limit to nearly everything; it is not surprising that man has not sought-out a conducive alternate environment to substitute (even as a war-time refuge), the one we still live in.

So, this compact book presents a fleeting glimpse and view on few current issues for which man's profitable use of his past experiences appears much questionable.

The first chapter (which follows the introductory commentary), is in an eccentric manner and mostly through an ecological lens (as with most of the following chapters); breezes through a historical example of how people can drastically review their terms of association with neighbours as their desired occasion arises. The second presents a sample of circumstances that should not be associated with freedom; like blackmail, financial system wickedness and use of religion to swindle people. The third chapter delves into a variety of features that in cross-boundary and territorial forms are plaguing society: examplified by obesity, political insensitivity, violent campaigns and a penchant for insincerity.

The fourth previews few aspects of human romance with contradictions. The fifth (which is the last of Part A), picture reviews a modern (Arab Spring) instance of abdication; which on regional comparative basis has a connotation of economic, human, material and infrastructural inadvertent wisdom.

The sixth to the ninth chapters which constitute the Part B, focus on few of man's interactions with; uses of and recent experiences with nature, in his environment. Which include but not limited to; issues of city floodings, adaptations of ideas from nature for mayhem and a catalogue of recent natural disasters suggestive of an epoch of changed patterns; probably linked to some issues of global-warming.

At the chapters' intervals, thought-provoking historic sayings and a few old poems of the author's, are added to spice-up the presentation. And a postscript commentary with a chronological listing of few natural disaster events of between September 2012 and mid-February 2013, closes the contribution.

E L Nwankwo

TABLE OF CONTENT

*In nature there are no rewards or
punishments; there are consequences*
(**Horace A Vachell** *1861-1955*)

*Nature has always had more
power than education*
(**Voltaire** *1694-1778*)

*Here is good advice for practice: go into
Partnership with nature; she does more than
half the work and asks none of the fee.*
(**Martin H Fischer** *1879-1962*)

INTRODUCTION

(A Culture of Calmness)

Seasons in the past came and left at definite times. In this era of distortions most of the traditionally predictable timings seem to have been shoved into a sac of relics; maybe a black-hole of sorts. So are we drifting onto a period of disorder? Or inducing the establishment of an era (maybe rather an epoch) of rapid chaotic changes?

Our musicals, worship sessions, festivals and more so, political gatherings have become more rowdy than wild hyena packs that are on a feeding frenzy. Our mega-cities' traffic commuting, is chaotic when compared with either the hurting match of soldier ants or even the dry seasons wild animals' Serengeti trek in East Africa. In our homes, juvenile, teenage, adult and parental disorderly conducts are often non- verbally encouraged. While the unleashing of unprovoked mindless murderous violence on an innocent public or bizarre arson, is apparently placated by groups seeking or preaching self-serving interests by advocating the importance of the human-rights of the perpetuators; apparently as the dead victims no-longer have any.

That peep into aspects of our troubling fields (with an ecologically biased lens) can if we will it, lead us to reinvigorate benefits that accrue from a noticeable culture of calmness. Yes; calmness because man's present state of affairs within all geographical boundaries, represents escalating disorder. As we induce circumstances, often as if there are no possibilities of even a natural reaction being triggered; we much more advertise our carelessness.

On the basis of that opinion, this slim volume presentation is in two parts, of nine chapters. The eccentric approach influences how the first part highlights few avoidable issues which today's man pilot's, regardless of his knowledge and better judgment. The second part: focuses on both few of his interactions with the ecosystem and a generalized peep into a period of what might be nature's compensatory reactions to man's years of sustained and inspired distortions. So the book includes:

- An example of motives and style of resource use.
- How self-desires over-ride wider concerns.
- irrespective of geographical boundaries some trends on the human body, religion, politics, violence etc; so easily relate to what ought to be odd.
- How more in the non-positive, human romance with contradictions thrives.
- How in a case of vice, a flash of common sense salvaged what history would quantify.

In continuation for the second part:

- Again, an example of motives of our use of the environment.
- A widespread repeated case type of short-changed modification of environment within cosmopolitan areas.
- A four part example of ecological issues (on: the big cats, termite colonies, animals' flight and seasonal migrations) that man draws lopsided inspiration from.
- an abridged catalogue of natural disasters highlight of April 2010 to Jan 2011 indicative of off-trend frequencies likely to herald a new epoch; having grounds to be associated with United Nations [UN] opinion focus on global warming.

In addition, at the beginning and end of many of the chapters; some sayings and poems have been added to provoke more thought and spice-up the compact presentation.

PART A

CHAPTER ONE

Cruelty has a human heart; And jealousy a human face

Terror the human form divine; And secrecy the human dress

-William Blake- (1757-1827)

A WAY OF MEN

The writer of the book 'Animal Farm', therein left scenarios to our imagination. Basic equality and a convergence of communal purposes; could be one of such. A studied peep into the biologically much eulogized termite ant-hill community, heinously disembowels most ideas of equity; though not like Anders Breivik, the mindless 2011 Norwegian mass murderer.

People epitomize ant-hills as lofty references of single purposed community with exemplary division of labour that brings about exceptional efficiency. The make-up therein remains; the queen and its drone, the soldiers and the workers. The sedentary queen sure meets her contributory quota by a prolific production of replacement batches of the caste's highly expendable worker termites. The soldiers in reality have little caste defending to ever, solely do and not much else either. Infact, under invasion or threat (as is with a porcupine's feeding visit), the workers are more suicidally used as a shield (reminiscent of the bizarre cases where civilians, women and children are used as human shields in some conflict situations). Within the caste though, the rest of the chores; obviously remains the worker-bees' responsibility. Any surprise then that in a copy-cat subtle desire, the famous Egyptians of Pharaoh's era, enslaved their refugeeing Israelite friends. Whom they ruthlessly 'tool-used'; for their never ending erection of pyramids. Magnificent ones, for powerful Pharaohs that reigned for long (like Ramses II who reigned 67years during the 19th dynasty); and even sizable one for King Tut that died a teenager. For a chute following of this jist with it's ecological, general ways of mankind and biblical slant; please like on a pop-up window of a laptop, hold the biblical pre-Moses rescue slavery account in picture. Most of all at this point, recall that the basic composition of those notable for driving the great pyramid era were; the Pharaohs, the soldiers and their slaves. Curiously, somehow in shape and internal design of chambers, the pyramids ideas must have been lifted from ant-hills. If so, any doubt that the idea of means of achieving the purposes would naturally come from a human adapted interpretation of how the termites organized their labour? Definitely the aim here is not to catalogue another idea probably from the ecosystem.

So let us think about it into modern times. For example, to an Arab Spring situation. Where else can be better than the cute land where the sunset over the Nile Rivera lets pyramids cast shadows over the landscape. The same Egypt? Yes the same Egypt. The bond between Pharaohs and their soldiers surely endures. Now without the privilege of slaves, the populace had to substitute. Oh!! the wave of democratic emotions came and somehow the citizens drove off pharaoh - sorry Mubarak. But they left off his backbone allies. Switch again briefly to the Bible; in response to a question, John the Baptist [a distant cousin of Jesus the Christ] in Luke chapter 3 verse 14 [NKJV], asked soldiers not to intimidate anyone, accuse falsely and be content with their wages. That was simply because they had a reputation and penchant of using false accusations and intimidation to disposes people of their belongings. [a common happening to

15

date in all nations]. On the part of being content with their wages, even in the 1970s and 80s, some contingents of UN peacekeeping forces were suspected of smuggling arms to both opposing warring factions for money.

This brings to light the views of a not-so sarcastic minority that the generation of African military Generals' heads of states deserve more empathy. These fellows [i.e.: of that era] when not 'gainfully' employed [ie, at war] or with 'Israelite type' of slaves to oppress, supposedly for a 'pharaoh-replica'; never let them near executive political office or over any form of national treasury. If in doubt ask any enlightened Nigerian above 45yrs and without links to such cliques. Else to the detriment of all, the scenarios for which the divinely inspired counsel of John the Baptist, would play out fully. They wage a private relentless annexation guerilla warfare on the Treasury contents. Would the national financial prosperity of these times in Germany and Japan have a thing to do with their not having a prominent contingent of such? As for USA, their recent republican presidents penchant of war-mongering abroad, may be serving an inadvertent associated domestic privilege. In addition to the cushion, checks and balances offered by their constitution, to resource access.

As we cast a closing glance into our termite anthill; a refreshing realization dawns, the so called defenders of castes, ought never be many.

So, without further stretching any of these yet elastic issues; what can be said to be new?

HUMAN CHARACTER

1. It takes wisdom to be patient

While pride requires emptiness to manifest.

2. It takes experience to appreciate hard work.

While the Lord shows inconfidence with boastfulness.

3. It takes sincerity to cultivate a healthy imagination

While it takes love for money to be a harbinger of disputes.

4. It takes good conduct to properly think

While it takes delinquent infancy to be rash.

5. It takes honesty to have simple desires

While greed is a manifestation of selfishness

6. It takes the experience of serenity to appreciate peace

While the blind passion for dominance and materialism

Precipitate holocausts.

7. It takes the discipline of thought to value life

While planlessness does not threaten the success

of destruction.

8. It takes the love of children to encourage growth

While it takes a mundanely meretricious

character to be unjust.

9. It takes the freewill of service to teach

While it takes an insipidly virulent mind to corrupt.

10. It takes comradeship to achieve progress

While a disordered laxity is a precursor to chaos.

ENYI-271286 (17.40HRS)

CHAPTER : TWO

Each one of us, in his timidity, has a
limit beyond which he is outraged.
-Man Ray- (1890-1976)

GLIMPSE ON TYRANNY OF FREEDOMS

Any who has run short of the knowledge of our cravings for limitlessness and lack of appreciation of our near irredeemable state of value decadence, has to be residing in planet Mars or far driven into recurring materials and drugs induced hallucinations. Materials desire, political power desire, monetary desire, dominion desire and a host of other types of desires purely blind to reason and given to greed, as such may now be competing for universal availability with atmospheric oxygen. If you even in the least imagine that to any degree, this is to poke fun, you could be under initial influence of the numbing influenza. Did I really mean influenza, when no medical vaccine exist for an antidote to the scourge? Or are there immune places, enclaves or domains? That, lamely suggests the possibility of existence of a non-contaminated precinct. Maybe a makeshift enclosure designated: a 'quarantine', for the more debilitated. Could an ideological practice incubate that? What of any modern religious lifestyle? Or could an undiluted cultural and traditional disposition foster such? Assuming all the previous fail; does the inadvertent lessons of our technology have a chance of stumbling on the like? Please do not whisper that the likelihood was actively fading with the questioning options.

The essence, purpose and or aim of this stirring lacks the privilege of advancing solutions based on arrogated experience. Far from such. After-all the intelligentsia, opinion leaders, generals, chieftains, as well as their enforcers and kingmakers, are not rationally expected to expunge an attribute describable as an equivalent of an author's qualification of religion being the opium of the masses.

As the title suggests, this is but a glimpse. Call it a 'birds eye view', to draw contentious debates or term it a selective highlight, to minimize stepping on too many toes; choices are now (ie: these days) often plastic but coated with a claim of being elastic. For a fact, liberties hinged on the diverse premise of freedom is not short of the bizarre on every platform. A few scenarios maybe illustrative:

 (a) A Prime minister or his designate tells representatives of another nation 'that their nation's continued benefit of aid would be dependent on a legislative enactment of statutes legalizing homosexuality and lesbianism'. The basis of the obscene and arrogant pre-condition being a worship belief of stretched tenets of equal rights activism. Meanwhile, historically over seventy five percent of the entire money value of the so-called aid somehow ends right back into the 'donor' nation's coffers and pockets of their nominated aid supervisors. For a more light on the depths and spread of the decadence; note that the involved political class has tacit collaborators in the mould of religious helmsmen of some sects who in one breath stand against same sex marriage and in another see nothing wrong with tolerating and ordaining homosexuals as bishops. We could term; a case of limitlessness induced by irrational democracy. Or could it be a type of cultural tyranny of freedom, since both hail from the same locality?

(b) In-case your association of the above conditional aid with tyranny is feeble; the exemplary highlight on few recent individuals' public gun violent massacres, ought to more clearly epitomize the tyranny of aspects of freedom. Due to comparable ease of access to information, reference on this would focus on recent American (USA) experience. Of the 15 major shootings in USA cataloged by Reuters news agency; from April 1999 (with the Columbine High School, Colorado massacre of 13) to the Dec 2012 (heinous slaughter of 20 kindergarten school kids aged 6 to 7years old in Newton, Connecticut, including 6 of their teachers), the more bizarre incidents have two common shocking features. First, the victims were positioned in public places and in no way (birth/parentage, belief or conduct) could have contributed to provocation for the act. Secondly, the crime scenes choice and timing of the premeditated violence resulted in high fatalities. While the July 2012 masked gunman attack at a movie theater in Denver, Colorado; in a way appears to be a modified copy-cat representation of the 2011 Norwegian killing madness by Andres Brievik, other high fatality incidents involved more of youth in 17 to 25yr age bracket. These well-armed gunmen, had some automatic assault weapons not legally theirs. The ease of acquiring arms and the loose restrictions on the multi-caliber assault rifle types coupled with the statutes in certain states that tacitly encourage their use (by the proviso likes of 'stand your ground'), fosters unusual freedoms for guns use. More so, as loosely defined freedom for defense is so often tyrannically switched for offense. As such the situation seems explainable but not understood. Prior to those, sorts of democratic tyranny or rather tyranny within freedom allowed numerically minor interest groups to effectively delay or block basic, essential and common sense proposed legislation in Congress or by selfish court process. A case in-point being the counter lobbying of National Rifles Association (NRA) and its affiliates in USA, for which it took that nation's Congress 7years (up till 1993) to pass a gun control bill (Brady Bill). Also, due to political considerations that nation's ban on categories of semi-automatic weapons that lapsed in 2004 remains unrenewed even in the aftermath of escalating unprovoked massacres. More especially by young fellows who could never have been provoked enough for a fraction of the senseless wickedness they commit.

 (c) Having browsed through an extremist type of tyranny made easier by loose freedom; recent happenings in banking financial cycles (particularly in Spain: where banks rescued from bankruptcy with taxpayers government funds, soon after embarked on ruthless low income public eviction loan recovery drives) would arguably portray a subtle resemblance to a form of tyranny that could be defended with sterile and otherwise polished clichés on legal freedoms, to so do. Secondly, in USA, the serious but comical struggle to increase tax on the 'rich' (of the apex 2%) has driven the squabbles to a time limit precipice, termed 'fiscal cliff'. Again, a case of individuals in numerical minority,(even though those are part of the elected representatives): were mounting a partly self-serving protectionist agenda for the well-connected but very few. Thirdly, the 2012 year-end British economic review realization, that their big firms were paying much less tax than they did 12 years ago (2000/01 income tax of £26 billion as against the current £21 billion) regardless of facts that companies' (both big and small) profitability had risen 65%, while the economy grew 55% over the same period (as reported by Reuters news agency, on the net (ie: on Thurs Dec27, 2012, 17.33 GMT).

 (d) For a measure of balance, a brief on the sly, the opportunistic and often the mean; as the happenings within religious cycles aptly demonstrates 'the tyranny of freedoms' in a variety of forms in both Christian and Muslim localities. Examples of which abound in Southeast Asia, the Middle-East, Africa, North and South America. Flocks are cajoled into many flabbergasting acts, including violence and blood-letting. The more modern and widespread pattern being the use of choice and restricted context quotations smoothly mired in oratory

21

grounded in techniques of mass hypnotism, to fleece the people of their money. A recent historical example of the previous, is the constitutional freedom in Guyana that enabled the violent killings and mass suicide of American Rev Jim Jones' flock by mid (18th) Nov 1978 in Jonestown, Guyana. For the present, recalling even the more spectacular episodes of religiously induced sectarian violence and the fleecing of huge sums of even borrowed money from the needy; would be both cumbersome and trite. Constitutional advantage, preference and liberties of different forms; have been exploited to enable and enhance the acts of tyranny.

That these pointer issues are not referenced to a single geographical location but more so within democracies of sorts; gives an indication of universal trend of disposition to veiled mockery of the base fabric of democracy. While that affirms 'the world now being a global village', crimes issues and the reluctance of restricting certain means of enabling such, as exemplified by the American guns control debates following the massacre of 20 kindergarten kids, fails to discountenance the impression that, socio-cultural factors still predisposes individuals to certain tendencies.

E L Nwankwo (Dec, 2012)

OH!! A TWISTED HEART

Long after the Sage said; seek ye beauty of the heart rather than the physical. A descendant shepherd added that; a maliciously contentious heart is not worth a missing swallow.

So:

- *When tears come and go without sobbing and brokenness*
  Beware a sly heart is at play.
- *When the sluggish at equity and flat-footed at empathy comes*
  Beware a wicked heart is lurking.
- *When selective memory is laced with a pious gait; oh!*
  Beware a slandering heart waits.
- *When ingratitude is concealed in self-justification*
  Beware a venomous heart seeks a victim.
- *When tale bearing is done with self-serving cynical twists*
  Beware a deceitful heart is preaching.
- *When repeated disputes combine with bouts of unfriendliness*
  Beware a polluting heart spreads rot.

ENYI-170107 (22.30HRS)

CHAPTER: THREE

The road to the city of
Emeralds is paved with
Yellow bricks.
-L. Frank Baun-(1856-1919)

Human folly is international
-Kurt Tucholsky-(1890-1935)

OVER-DRIVE WAVES

[Some Borderless Trends]

The internet age packs a lot of loads. Many that reinforce the enduring wisdom of old titles like 'the good; the bad and the ugly'. It has long become synonymous with imputing of numerous extra and mostly farfetched meanings to both words and terms. So, for the title 'over-drive waves', the perceptions could well differ not only with the localities but even the time of the day and age group of the person. A decade ago, the urbane would grin as the thoughts of a new sporty 5-speed geared car driven to an ocean-side resort during a weekend, flashes to the mind. Today, such unrestricted public places are mostly story books issues worldwide. For sure; in Europe, USA or Africa, day or night, at a local public cinema or an island youths' political rally; innocent gatherings become mindless mass killing fields. So our waves of violence, be it the sporadic individual madness or own communal slaughterings [the Arab Spring models] or the infamous Bosnian ethnic cleansing; not missing-out the religious toned 'boko haram' insanity in northern Nigeria, all turn man into his own hostage. The wave-like spread of this malaise across all forms of boarders may justify coining an appropriate description borrowing phrases or connotations from pandemic and revolution. For a simple reminder; when a movement is on 'over-drive', it has to be cruising with less effort, thus the likelihood of an added wavelike rocking.

So far, this may already be sounding to some as an exercise in use of English. We humbly crave your indulgence not to so conclude; for the facts would annul that. Not so 'short' commentaries on about six simple and common everyday issues, would be used to highlight the phenomenon alluded to. As it is said that 'charity begins at home' we can chose to begin the panoramic review with an issue of the human body.

MEDICAL

Obesity is the sole issue of choice here. The reasons of this are that this condition is not: sex limited or related, nor transmitted like an infectious disease or genetically inherited. Please before the gun trotting 'quick-draws' pull out their AK47s (for which, North African Arab-spring leftovers are reported selling cheap); a brief on what obesity really is. From; www.medicalnewstoday.com :when a person's body has accumulated so much body fat that it may have a negative effect on the health; an obese condition is said to exist. The person's body mass index [BMI] has to be 30% or more; those with a BMI of 25-29.9% are only classed as over-weight but not obese. Research findings quoted therein for USA, claims that because of over eating, that 14% of that nation was obese in 1980 and in 2000, 31%. In 1971, their women averagely ate 1542 calories daily; 1877cal by 2004. Their men ate 2450cal and 2618cal for the same years respectively. The increases composed more of carbohydrates from processed foods dished by fast foods outlets. Those being cheaper than fruits and vegetables, was said to have encouraged the shift in meal types. Eating habits that disrupt metabolism and sleeping less aids fat accumulation. However, the now prevalent leading of more sedentary lifestyles [with TV, computers, video games, remote controls, washing machines and excessive use of vehicles- even for 5-10 minute walking distances] much induces the condition. The above factors responsible for this wave of problematic, odd and disproportionate waist-line increases is not confined to USA but noticeable as being on the rise also in Nigerian urban centres. A nation where food is not enough for popular over eating but processed carbohydrates use, has become rampant [both in and out of fast-foods outlets]. Sadly, medicare access and costs in the later class of locality is of serious concern. More so as one of obesity's main health risks is osteoarthritis, for which women are said to be nine times more predisposed to.

Public attitude towards it (obesity), appears to be more of stressed tolerance than empathy; not, acceptance in many localities. So, disgust with public parade of disproportionate waist-line increases in recent years has not always been subtle. In a show of dwindling patience with the unsavory image it creates for organisations, many Police commands and precincts of Thailand, Pakistan, Britain, Indonesia and Philippines are known to have ordered their pot-bellied and obese traffic officers off the roads, to get fit or shed 'the sacs' before they return to work. Gosh!! The issue to follow is one made sacred for ages by men more for; the benefits, fanning the egos of, and in subtlety perpetually maintaining allegiance of the flock, to the arrowheads. Surely; religion.

RELIGION.-

Presently religious practices are so much around, religion needs neither classification nor description for a big picture overview of one of it's related factors. While the principal issue is not to x-ray it's workings but as was with medical issue, a mere highlight of an associate condition on people regardless of geographical boundaries. Proliferation of sects and establishment or incorporation of private organizations under this umbrella is the focus. The Christian fate has a rich historical reference on this. While grudge reference to the mainly European inquisition over a century ago persists as an underlying remote cause factor, the present 'wildfire spread style' of the phenomenon has been claimed to be traceable to the following:(a) unbridled leadership ambitions (b) high-handedness and brazen injustices by both none and the orthodox leaderships (c) greed (d) platform for fanaticism arising from political inequalities and (e) lack of employment of sorts; among others. The imports of some of the above, is obvious in the sectarian civil crisis presently in the Muslim dominated Middle-east [where in particular, Syria is an Alawite/Sunni war theater]. In-light of that, it is worth mentioning that Rana Kabbani (a Syrian Historian) wrote that 'fundamentalism is a specter that is stalking the globe .....'; few years before this wave of Arab Spring. For a spotlight in Asia, India's wide religious diversity [as replicated in Nigeria to a lower extent] has not fostered any form of sustained unity or advantage.

Next is the turf on which; from which and with which unending historical troops of mavericks are made and nakedly cleaned-out. You guessed right: politics.

POLITICS

This diverse mine field from whichever point of view and wherever; that now menacingly but like a sly giant squid stalks every fabric of society, would be made contact with (i.e.: commented on) only on account of insensitivity. This perverse attitude often in exotic urbane flair, where freedom of speech is saturated with much self (or rather selfishness and self-centeredness); is usually in the guise of party, regional or national interests. Reports on the recent workings of the chambers of the United Nations (UN) bare much of this imprint. The facts on the plights of humans appears less seriously attended to than those of endangered species. Infact, in the present fascist international diplomatic arena, irony and sarcasm because of their subtle suggestion of intellectual superiority is flaunted in occasions where a party is chanced with a clear moral higher ground, rather than due priority attention given to the pressing matter. Events of months of actual inertia on the Arab Spring matters refers. The wave of apparently infectious insensitivity habit gets to some national, regional and local assemblies (i.e.; houses of political representatives) as well. Some have on occasions been reported to have on grounds of assumed sacrosanct 'house procedure order' failed to consider urgent matters that touch on survival and wellbeing of sections of the citizens they represent. That has been so even with a voiced protest. Some victims of natural/extreme weather disasters, religious and communal skirmishes have been additionally shocked by such. Truly, while some types of unanimism helps out with individual pettiness, it's insensitive pitfall of assuming that majority is always right will continue to be plagued by historic shameful examples.

To conveniently follow politics is liberty; just like the presentation of the flip side of a coin.

LIBERTY

Unlike for the preceding issues for which highlights focused on single aspects, here it would be spread into; entertainment, dialogue and campaigns of violence. Much of this reference liberty is a consequence of forms of democratic freedom boosted by the reach and rapidity of information technology.

For **[a]: Entertainment**; fashion and music would be more than enough components representation. The similarities in their courses of change, driving forces and their mechnics, as well as their main promoters; encouraged this collective brief. While fashion, more refers to clothing that is in vogue at a particular time and place; a description of music meant to avoid contending ideological leanings, says it is an artful arrangement of sounds across time. Though the purpose is obvious to the concerned, so also is that music definition vague to many with scientific mindset. Both fashion and music have rich histories. While William Shakespeare in 16th century wrote that 'fashion wears out more apparel than the man'; Confucius in ancient China believed that only the superior man who can understand music is equipped to govern. An indication, to their historic association with rapid change and the powerful. Critiques have claimed that sheepish adherents to fashion are frivolous, immoral and irrational; while their designers bring about rapid changes for greedy gains. That background and its tenets rather than change, has in a wavelike form and on a worldwide scale rapidly mutated and spread. Information technology facets (radio, TV, computers and internet) with their reach and rapidity, aided and established a new rebellious generation of 'do your own thing' to bring about extraordinary cliques of adherents and artists. So, without further elaboration (ie: to avoid being harshly critical) the spread of the current vogue of some dress fashion and video-music, which is hoped to be a short-lived fad, alludes to the discuss phenomenon. If you are reading this late in 2012 or not long after; then you would remember the saggy loose fitting out-fits of many urban young adult males and the brief upper laps-exposing close fitting skirts with correspondingly short, low necked tops that give a clearly unsolicited view of bursts' cleavage as well as the stomach navel of many more females. A craze made more bizarre (ie:

to some), by the 'small' league of middle-aged female converts. Most of whom, a dare to dialogue on the issue would make them rant and rain unqualified abuses.

[b] Dialogue: here, not 'freedom of speech', is the intriguing issue of choice. The later, more of an exclusive turf on which journalists have been enjoying swinging maneuvers with their barely acknowledged partners- politicians; is an ancient graveyard requiring catharsis by another, therein experienced. Dialogue rather represents what nearly all of society is routinely involved in. Within dialogue, the issue is a new wave of people of all works of life often habitually displaying con-men tendency. They side-step on facts and with subtle ease distort the truth - the basic working operational mechnics of: spin. That verb with more than a dozen meanings or connotations, like the word clique (because of few 'not so good' meanings), has acquired a negative general reference. Three of those for spin, form the basis of this. They would include:[i] to give biased information - i.e.; present facets of information in a way meant to direct the influence of others [ii] invent story -i.e.; to diversify a story or a series of lies [iii] twist public opinion -i.e.; relate a story or remark in contexts to serve selfish ends or even cast a web of hazy understandings to the facts. As such euphemism plays in spin's league. Many may for face-saving purposes claim it is an inborn man's habit, as even toddlers use wailing to blackmail their parents to accede to repeat requests- not only for hunger. The claim also that the use of spin cuts across the social fabric and of all age groups, does not explain or justify its current widespread and much use. That most politicians in government routinely put spins to 'explain' spurious doings, even to the disgust of discerning teenagers, is no longer new. The fascinating, is the rampant use of such by the now many sly professionals [including but not limited to: publicists, lawyers, stockbrokers, bankers, marketers, some religious preachers and medical

30

scientists]. Those now often con segments of society with claims on trends that they in time may reverse with equally dubious intents. Reminiscent of the mercurial part-time and roadside artisans (particularly the automotive types) of many nations. That may give an insight as to why society tends to have become much more permissive (ie: because it has so often been repeatedly shocked unto numbness) on the failures of its political leaderships - even on account of violent acts.

[c] **Campaigns of violence**: Like the use, applications and varied components nature of spin, violence as well as the campaigns of it, is diverse. Though violence can be briefly described as physical attack on another person; other known traumatic but non-physical forms also constitutes issues of concern. It has even been classed into legal and illegal forms or types. The legal forms include the likes of sports (e.g.: boxing, martial arts), haunting and even law enforcement. Some occasionally organized forms of illegal violence include: assault, rape, robbery, duress (siege) and homicide. Other forms are; cases of political and ethnic violence (e.g.: pogrom), also cases of sustained feuds and vendetta between families or organizations. As such, all forms of family/domestic violence is not within the scope of this. To some, theories on violence are within three main schools of thought. First, Sigmud Freud and co, who believe violence is inherent in man. Then, the French Philosophers who rather assert that aggression is not inherent in man but learned. The third (like John Dollard and co) say; aggression is always a result of frustrations. However from a biological perspective; hereditary and behavioral studies show that all other primates are particularly not much aggressive and lack the lust to kill; much unlike man. The flux of varied degrees of acceptance or association with those ideological inclinations has given rise to many assertions. While cultural disposition,

experiences and present circumstances are base factors that characterize reactions of people; some so claim that many violent campaigns arise from the quest for liberty of varied forms or sorts. Even in times past, the belief was that most violent campaigns arose as a rebellion against inhuman acts. The 1680 Pueblo Rebellion, synchronized by the natives against Spanish missions and garrisons, is a historic example on that. Yet others now also complain that liberty does give room for frivolous violent acts. To go through such a maze of reasonings may require a series. The focus is however limited to giving a fleeting view on an aspect of the trend's spread, regardless of ideological and or physical boundaries. That is so, more restricted to the illegal episodes of sieges (in the mould of assault and homicide), organized feuds and vendettas, as well as political and ethnic attacks. A sample listing of worldwide examples of such would include:

- anti-foreigners violence in Germany

- ethnic violence in Burundi & Bosnia

- Islamic fundamentalism

- abortion clinics & Ku Klux Klan attacks in USA.

Just as family/ domestic violence has been screened out, so also at this point goes: national economic territorial disputes like; as in South China Sea (involving China, Japan and the Philippines) and the Faulkland Islands in South America (involving Britain and Argentina). But part of all this, is also to show that inspite of comparative knowledge explosion (i.e.; within this decade, that ought to much more humble man; make him vastly empathetic and purge much of the lust for violence), the reverse is the case. From internet tutoring, the production of 'home made' explosives and dirty bombs has been used to make insurgencies, feuds and ethno-political violence most vicious, rampant and widespread. While it maybe quite trite to list the phenomenon's spread (for prominent examples of most, dot all the continents), it has become shameful to recall that just as the discovery of theory of relativity was more quickly and elaborately used for evil; the internet did not chart a different course. In that light, it's overall contributions since 2010 to date for the following is outstanding:

-   in South America; the Colombian drugs cartel wars.

-   Middle East (Arab Spring); ethno-political rebellions and   pogrom-like manslaughters.

-   Europe and North America; mindlessly bizarre individual rampages (eg: the Andes Breivk 2011 Norwegian youth's massacre)

-   Asia, Africa and Middle-east; Islamic fundamentalism (eg: Boko-haram insurgency in northern Nigeria)

Much more widespread and rampant than the above (as such issues being grappled with by many nations) are: workers' protests which turn violent (eg: the August 2012 South African platinum mine human massacre).

To sum-up, we briefly wind-back to the 'good, bad and ugly' reference in the opening. The odds of the highlights favored only the bad and the ugly. Surely 'the goods' exist but in a serious minority and made apparently insignificant by the scale and extent of the others. However, in respect of the tenets of equity, the following is also mentioned, for that:

-   In the few places where food is within the reach of many, the people appear to be healthier though violence related stresses still lurk near homes.

- While information technology has much helped the spread of religious knowledge, infiltration of fundamentalism remains a snag.

- The massive political platforms and relative freedom, has aided stress bursting freedom of expression (irrespective of taints by violent acts).

- Varied facets of entertainment has used the platform of information super-highway to extraordinarily boost youth employment and encourage private entrepreneurship.

Yet, the contributions of the bad and the ugly facets remain (maybe not numerically so but still) overwhelming.

Sorry, yet sure !!!

E L Nwankwo. (Aug/Sept 2012)

[d] DIALOGUE : 2

SPINS; CONS and FIBBING

[What's the difference?]

Many citizens asked to stop at road shoulders often fail to 'fib' (an almost colloquial term for telling a veiled lie of convenience: in some dictionaries, simply referred to as; untrue statement) themselves out of the traffic encounter with the police.

Also for ages, most politicians in government routinely put a spin (ie: to present in a distorted and hazy manner, that actually falsifies), to explain spurious doings, which disgust even discerning teenagers.

Just as our new breed [20th century and later], sly professionals [lawyers, stockbrokers, marketers, some religious preachers and even medical scientists] regularly con (knowingly and colourfully use half-truths to deceive) the society with claims on trends that they in time reverse with equally dubious intents.

The youth who are most involved with the fibbing incidents with the police, have been for almost an age spiritedly tutored [non-verbally] by their parents, guardians and mentors; who include more than those already mentioned. The political office holders ever dependent on spin, sly professionals who eloquently find excuses for their opinions, as well as 'holier than thou' journalists [print and electronic], all daily and at every turn stuff youngsters with running examples of smooth and camouflaged falsehood. As hypocrisy provides extraordinary hindrance to basic discipline and good judgment; permissiveness in homes has become rampant. So much so that even toddlers now, more seem to use wailing to blackmail their parents to accede to repeat chocolate and candy requests.

Maybe most do not even realize this malaise cuts across the social fabric and age groups. It is already mentioned of societal conning by some preachers. Also, spins more associated with politicians seem to be traditionally useful to the arrow heads of some religious groups. An author's gift copy of the book 'Proliferation of Churches' in 2010 let me deduce the opinion that dogmatic self-serving interpretations of the scriptures can be associated with denominational doctrines. Can spin be much more elegantly subtle than that?

While not positioning for any sort of endorsement of propaganda; which is related to, but not a Siamese twin of these issues; that has truly also, found expressions not only for war-time use but into the much slime world of diplomacy, sleazy boardrooms of organized sports and reprehensive leadership caucuses of religious organizations. Surely, very strong qualifying words; but fair and deserved if you have been on the receiving-end of the maneuvers of any of those. Infact, which modern human tragedy [not triggered by a natural disaster like earthquake, landslides or tsunami] is not traceable to at least one of those? Actually the focus here lies elsewhere.

If anyone, in sincere ignorance wonders how and why organized sports made such an exclusively shameful list; briefly cast your mind to the recent reports on international professional cycling. 'The most professional, extensive, elaborate and successfully organized drugs-use cheating episode in history'. A fair rephrase of one of the reports' descriptive summation, on the cycling disgrace. Indeed, 'con-men par excellence'. Any difference between those and the obviously barely pretentious gangs of world-wide wrestling federations (WWF)? Or would it take additional evidence to convince a few more? Fair enough: a little further the memory lane but briefly; incidents of anabolic steroids use in the Olympics by members of some weightlifting teams. So would the organizations, institutions and or governments tacitly responsible for sponsoring such, be expected to morally and successfully stand against plagiarism, copyright violations, exams malpractices; for which the more involved age brackets are close? The same reference age grades also more watch TV and use the internet. So much has been written and said on the decadence and corrupting influence traceable to both media- the modern undisputed champion tools for information dissemination and propaganda. The echo of the saying that: 'you cannot eat your cake and have it' thus resonates. A wrap-up at that point, would give the wrong impression that the insinuated age bracket solely holds sway in those.

Rather, it appears to replicate the history of industrial incidents scenerio; where the number of near-miss incidents far belittle or make insignificant those of fatal disasters. Meanwhile the severity and consequences of the later, tends to make it trivial to have the previous on any reportables' lists. For this, a recent classical historical illustration may suffice. A decade ago (about 19th March 2003), the army of USA, along with a smaller British contingent invaded Iraq. Prior to that; repeated, long and massively occastrated rhetoric insistence by George W Bush (the then American President) and his eloquently able collaborator Tony Blair (then British Prime Minister), claimed that Iraq's Saddam Hussein's government had weapons of mass destruction, to justify the invasion. Those two leaders used the powerful media propaganda machines allied to their political parties (much against the weakly expressed feelings of majority of their nations' citizens) for the hype based on supposed security and intelligence reports. Against worldwide and extensive appeals, pleas and protests (even requests within the corridors of UN, for just an extra 2 weeks of more diplomatic efforts), were brashly ignored as the invasion was launched. Eventually, no weapon of mass destruction was ever found. Not even a tail-tell sign of any in the past (ie; physical forensic evidence). So, at the least; a historical tsunami of fraud, hoax and perculiar lies (or rather sustained load of spin and con) was used to excuse a motive. A second and 10th year anniversary report by; Watson Institute for International Studies at Brown University (USA), on the Iraq war, as packaged in Reuters.com web reports of Thurs. 14th Mar 2013; among others, states that:

- the war killed at least 134,000 civilians. And could have well, contributed to the death of over 500,000.

- USA gained little; with a veterans' medical and disabilities claims of $33 billion as at 2011.

- Iraq was traumatized.

- It reinvigorated radical Islamic militants of the region.

- It set-back women's rights and weakened frail healthcare of the region.

- The $212 billion reconstruction funds, was a colossal failure (most of the money spent on security; lost to wastes and fraud).

While it may still take some years for a reliable, independent and neutral assessment of or quantification of the human and materials disruption and losses within Iraq presents a more 'balanced' picture. So, much more than what Frederick II (1712-1786) said (that 'it is a political error to practice deceit, if deceit is carried too far') remains at play in this circumstance.

As obvious from the said Iraqi issue, the build-up and thereafter; involved desperately copious use of a mix of spin, con and fibs. Currently and more so in high drama diplomatic circles (as well as some party politics and governmental events), the use of spin, counter-spin and rolled-over maze of spin layers has resulted in claims on occasions that, a problem of attempting to disabuse the minds of some, of a conspiracy theory gets stone-walled by the fact that their argument becomes an extension of the conspiracy process. In those circumstances also, a mute response quickly confirms a non-verbal admission of guilt.

The sub-title, so finds grounds to question the difference between spin, con and 'fibs'. The issues also led to the mention of propaganda. Circumstances of use rather than the user's age or sex is a relevant factor. Social standing and location may increase use frequency rather than which. A colourfull and maybe fitting analogy of the differences can be taken from the auto-industry. The earlier reference as Siamese babies connotes a single parentage; while propaganda ought be an influential relative or sibling. Toyota and or Volkswagen is appropriate. Both within the same year models make cars of varied body designs [shapes] but with the same chassis. As well as making medium sized Sports Utility vans [SUV], which use the same engines of some of their salon cars.

So, some may regard the differences; fundamental, others class them; cosmetic. Like the vehicles, they have a common manufacturer and take their commuters [users] to their choice destinations. Similarly as well, while some cities grapple with peculiar polluting effects of vehicles' carbon emissions [just as the now ubiquitous falsehoods of 'spin' and co remain undesired], palliative measures to contain the stressors continue. Regrettable however, is the fact that for every organism in all environments [not different for man], there is always a limit dependent on some [known and unknown] factors [relevantly termed 'the carrying capacity'], following which an un-manageable catastrophic decline process sets-in, for that population. Rather than such dramatic manifestation, other resultant responses are subtle yet efficiently thorough. So, we will surely get to the limit of our tolerance and use of spin, con and fibbing.

E L Nwankwo. (March 2013)

CHAPTER: FOUR

CONTRADICTIONS

(On few views of humanity's expanding scar)

The virtues of civilization are incompatible with civic virtues.
(**Ernest Gellner** 1925-1995)

Contradictions if well understood and managed can spark off the fires of invention.
(**Chinua Achebe** 1930-2013)

The last section of the previous chapter has a subtitle that questions the differences between a group of three vices scourging the fabric of society. The distinctions though explicit grammatically too few; is practically for us all on the street, purely esoteric. That is more so as all such life issues give rise to a variety of direct and indirect consequences. The more durable of which defy geographical boundaries, enlightenment and even to an extent time limitations. The focus here is for a fleeting review commentary on: Contradictions, which fits the brief. Just as it is said that 'the cat has nine lives', this issue (of contradictions) has derived an array of resilient auxiliary (survival) life factors from what experienced use of spin and con particularly, induces.

Unlike some other words that have a wide variety of connotations; the not too many dictionary meanings of this are distinct. That given by Merriam-Websters dictionary and thersus as 'a situation in which inherent factors, actions, or propositions are inconsistent or contrary to one another', much describes the perspective of this overview. Also, the first of the two descriptions given by Encarta Dictionaries (2009) as 'something that has aspects that are illogical or inconsistent with each other', equally suits this commentary. Aspects of human endavours like education, religious views, social dispositions, political practices, environmental and even medical science opinions, have hosted forms of illogicalities or inconsistencies. So, they come often masked, camouflaged or veiled with a variety of guises. Political situations, academic postulations, religious practices and even social opinions, at the least provide the festering grounds for this expanding human scar. Moreso, regrettably and contrary to basic expectations; today's enlightenment and technological advancement, seem to have within no human dwellings provided a shred of insulation from the pains inflicted by this expanding human scar. Not even a suggestion on how to scale-back the rate of its painful erosion, let alone an insight to any dependable restorative means. If that is a subtle preamble, it weaves the use of contrasts through most of what constitutes the broad spectrum of man's everyday life endeavors. Presently, a seemingly glowing era of: contradictions galore and contradictions extraordinary.

Here, we can only peep onto a tip of its iceberg; sectors of which represent the broad spectrum of our doings. For example, the now often justifiable and common occasions of alerting governments, stakeholders and the public on instances of threat to the environment; by some Ecologists (in a veiled copy-cat replication of the high decibel frenzied hype of computer marketers in 1999 to herald the new millennium), over-state the sensitivity and difficulties to recovery of indicator species, as well as the potential for floral and faunal re-colonization of devastated environments. When convenient (within the confines of tertiary institutions), the same professionals also do lecture that nature; regardless of man's perturbing interferences, provides for balanced ecosystems (with even interwoven webs of prey-predator sustainable exploitations). Contentions within the ranks of their first cousins; Evolutionary biologists, on a myriad of issues (few of which include: pre-historical extinctions reasons, questionable practicality of the big bang theory and the likes), appear more associated with the clauses of the second definition.

Contrary to the impressions of age-long accommodation of divergent opinions, enhanced by dynamism of knowledge development; what is more real is that in some instances, the agreed opinions of cartel-like groups, rather assumes the position of entrenched facts. Though the need to expanciate, for emphasis is here restricted; a quick reminder points to the criticism, harassment and assaults suffered by those that postulated that the world is spherical, during a previous century. Even some of the then clerical arrow-heads joined the persecution by branding it (the suggestion that the world was spherical): tantamount to heresy. So, opinions that run counter to the interests of real and or quasi authority figures (governmental, religious, academic, traditional, cliques, gangs and cartels alike) have historically often been quashed. A historical example of an event in West Africa (Nigeria) would suffice. In the said case, less than ten colonial officers whose presence (despite an earlier notice; not to come) disrupted a solemn tradition of ancient Benin kingdom, so got killed; the British colonialists declared it as a terrible massacre. Their swift and awful retaliatory guns aided slaughter of hundreds within that kingdom remains gleefully referred to as an 'expedition' by some historians. Based on such that continues to repeat in many different forms worldwide; an author recently serialized an article on government having a monopoly of violence. That has actually acquired universal empathy, founded on acceptance of a classification of violence, which includes: boxing, haunting, martial arts and armed law enforcement, as legal forms of violence.

So, even when a majority openly and for an extended period sustains views or acts (no matter how innocuous), that are inimical to interests of the authorities (as is the present Syrian situation, that has precipitated into a civil war), armed law enforcement violence; (which is a legal monopoly of the government), is used to silence the irritant. Realistically, many rightly wail. But that is as if it is new or a convenient blind eye had not been severally turned on more confined but similar numerous minor cases. Which re-enforces the applicable accuracy of the age-long and times-proven adage of industrial safety professionals that, 'it is the pack of ill-attended near-miss incidents at the bottom of the pyramid that eventually precipitates the disaster at the peak'. Surely, that would still only make sense to few, by choice.

For a bit of balance and avoidance of undue exoneration of our past systems, a brief exemplary reference is made from the 12th century. 2009 Microsoft Encarta Premium credits French Philosopher Peter Abelard of that era, with revolutionizing teaching methods by use of contradicting texts formats. That was a clear departure from the medieval styles of the Sophists and Jesuits (ie; the clever oratorials by the likes of Socrates and use of repeats to foster understanding; respectively for both ideological blocks). However, a later group of critical scholars (after Abelard), did not overhaul the style; rather carefully insert teleguiding resolutions to the issues. In a form of subtle endorsement of use of contradictions, Gilbert Highet's vintage book 'The Art of Teaching' gave the opinion that, from even medieval times there was the tendency to ground knowledge by expository understanding of contrasts. It further did add that, many regard Jesus Christ as the most famous teacher, and is known to have much used both parables and analogy of contrasts to effectively teach. In effect, it can be said that contradictions has deep roots also in our learning systems.

So, on occasions, even analogies can help scope issues for better appreciation of 'fluid' circumstances. When a veiled replication of a monastery (maybe not quite similarly located in remote confines), provides for willful co-habitation of the presumed saintly and his renown antagonist; a breeding nest of contradictions has been weaved. When theater performances depict scenes of simultaneous contrasting commotion; a mockery of societal contradictions is made. When we stretch our limits of permissiveness into uncharted precincts, on the guise of democratic purity, unadourable contradictions sprout on our drive-way. Satires, to many were tasteful and ever suitable for African moon-light folklore tales. Today however, the emerging scenarios of American and West European democracy; at the least, eulogizes some behavioral aberrations. Media hype and glittering rhetorics of women's affirmative action provided lead foot-prints for gay rights and expectedly copy-cat sequential legalizations of 'same-sex marriages'. Hopefully, we may yet get a perceptible glimpse of the basis for the maze of the contradictions. Nations where their female population components are out-stripping that of males, still widely consider it obscene and as such legally unacceptable to endorse polygamy. A position derived from the teaching of the New Testament section of the Bible :(a 66 books document), which a significant number of Americans want legally kept away from the public. In many of such nations, there is considerable legal tolerance of females who resort to violence on account of their male partner being involved with another female. To further give examples on those chain of occasionally clownish contradictions, reference is made of an April 26, 2013 web (www) report; that an incarcerated prisoner in a Baltimore (USA) jail; fathered five kids with four different female guards of his confinement facility.

As if a hallmark of today's society includes limitlessness even for the bizarre; a more heinously outrageous rolls reversal-event, was revealed on Monday 6th

May 2013. Which was that three young ladies (M Knight, A Berry and G DeJesus) kidnapped in 2002, 2003 and 2004 respectively in Cleveland, USA by a former school bus driver (Ariel Castro), with the assistance of a neighbour had been rescued. During the captivity, the victims were repeatedly raped, abused, starved and beaten to forcefully induce miscarriages; yet neighbours of the closely built-up area knew nothing of the decade long saga.

A simplistic suggestion based on what has been stated, ought to be that; same-sex coupling was better for the 'extra' ladies in light of the 'scarce' or 'dwindling' reproductive adult males populations. If so, same-sex marriage should be restricted to females. That same Bible provision, on which polygamy is discouraged; rather vehemently also abhours same-sex intercourse relationships. It describes the later; as an act of depraved minds. A clearly very strong qualification.

Tracking back a little for clarity; a less fuzzy model of democracy that is decided on not being much associated with lukewarm tendencies; could aid female same-sex coupling and encourage the likes of four different female guards making five or even more babies with their confined stud. After-all, man is an avid copy-cat; the idea of use of a suitably confined male, could have been a rather poor adaptation from the norm within termite anthill colonies. On the contrary, letting matters be; suggests we continue to 'comfortably' live a horde of gradually increasing issues of odd, curious and often bizarre contradictions.

That may not suggest a farfetched opinion; as the given, only represents a meagre sample of the issues. The following highlight a few more:

-       World popular advocacy of Privacy; beside large scale demands of extensive personal details on electronic database forms. That is regardless of the fact that, that has provided a good platform for fraud (especially financial types) by varied levels and forms of computer hacking.

- UN declarations of nations' Sovereignty viewed against its security council's positional acts on prevention of nuclear proliferation; permanency of its membership and structural mechnics of the veto it wields, all share not much with the perspective and or depth of some western democracy tenets. Unless, institutionalized double standards is its new preferred mode of non-member engagements.

- Curious statutory encouragements of homosexuality; about a decade ago said to enhance spread of acquired immune deficiency syndrome; by the gleeful legalizations of same sex unions on the flimsy excuse of sacrosanct fundamental human rights; yet euthanasia on all grounds and polygamy are protested.

Any Wonder then that a violent militant advocacy group (Boko-haram) would go by a philosophy that western education is bad; yet it uses internet based tutoring to fabricate 'dirty' bombs/explosives; which they use for dastardly acts. Most often on a segment of the innocent public (referred to as 'soft targets' by security agencies).

- More on United Nations' 'difficulties', could further illustrate. Established in 1945 to supersede the failed League of Nations but now embroiled in debilitating progressive internal contradictions, seems to be headed into a vicious extinction cycle. The implementation of the lofty ideals of its Article 1(part of what all member states endorsed), appears rudimentary. While often, the more powerful and arms supplier nations, for selfish economic reasons; disregard, abuse and violate Item no.s 4 and 5 of Article 2. Those often in practice, sort of has lead the UN to assume the position of the intelligent subordinate rather than the wise manager; that maximizes delegation as an added means of enhancing team building, as such resolving conflicts before they arise. That is going by the over 100year old counsel of Du Mu (in the book 'The Art of War' by Sun Tzu), that leaders ought to exploit the fact that: the intelligent are glad to establish their merit; the brave act-out their ambitions; the greedy welcome an opportunity to pursue profit and the foolish fail to care to die. In effect, the contradictory hindering play of greedy and self-acclaimed brave nations disrupt peace processes in conflict regions usually involving at least one egocentric or foolishly deceived combatant party. All for which, the news media report that the locally affected victim populations thus occasionally question the relevance of the UN. While those who are quick to deride and or trivialize the media raised issues, do so on the basis of opinions such as those of Marshall Mc Luhan's (1911-1980), that 'a point of view can be a dangerous luxury when substituted for insight and understanding'.

- As already indicated, even the entertainment industry has long cashed-in on the observation; much so that not only 'stand-up' comedians make a treat out of the issues. Maybe not few would have forgotten the satirical comedy movie (Trading Places) starred by Eddie Murphy and Dan Aykrody, though for entertainment, actually laid bare the vanity, triviality and unnecessary issues of contradictions of aspects of our value systems.

While the given list of simple, as well as the embarrassing circumstances is not exhaustive but just a replica of a statistical sample; it is noteworthy to add that the penchant neither respects geographical boundaries nor is it more associated with any modern social classes. Obviously therefore, as years roll-by, some of the absurd trends tend to blossom on a sort of bandwagon effects. That made me better understand why on an occasion years past, my Dad pointed-out that 'blatant arrogance is a sure foundation on which history cynically repeats itself". Which may underscore, why the current British Prime Minister (David Cameron) in 2012 did canvas (infact, on occasions during a tour of some African nations tried subtle arm-twisting) for legalizing of same sex marriages. In the process of which his aides were so fascinated, they could not remind him that his host audience still remembered the opinions of: Edward Heath (an ex-British PM), that 'he does not think that modesty is the outstanding characteristic of contemporary politics'; Ely Culbertson (a US bridge player), that 'power politics is the diplomatic name for the law of the jungle'; and Thomas Mann (a German Writer), that '...politics and the belief in it makes men arrogant, doctrinal and inhuman'. Eventually, a British Parliamentary bill for same-sex marriage was slated for debate during the 3rd week of May 2013. A bill said to be or widely regarded and referred to as one of Cameron's flagship bills. The gentleman (using a British parliamentary cliché) happens to be happily married to a female and cuts the image of a potential casanova. So, his zealous quest on that issue gives the impression of 'man on a mission' or personal life ambition; chanced with his party's support; yet contrary to his practical values. Incidentally not to be out-done and reminiscent of the past era's race to the moon; out-spoken and flamboyant neighbours across the English channel (the French) steamrollered their own same sex marriage legislation and their President Francois Hollande promptly signed it into law on 18th May 2013 (i.e.: the week before the British version's parliamentary debate). So, the question arising from the perplexing weird contradiction on and to values, pressing needs, exigencies, importance and relevance; is what direct and or indirect, immediate, short or long term benefits (on their economy, improvements of infrastructure, health, security, communications and or even education; alternatively better costs reduction with improved dispensation of justice) would the hype and sustained rhetoric on the same sex coupling quest (much against Christian, Muslim, Hindu, traditional Asian, South American and African/Middle-East belief systems) beneficially serve any nations or humanity? Infact, even the largely atheist nation of China customarily has no place for the same-sex fad. Unlike most of the other issues beset with contradictions that sprouted from deeply set roots of greed or group ego, this is neither traceable to such nor should it be excused by fancy flimsy reasons. A reverend gentleman (who to avoid being politically wrong and in some conflict with his bishop), said 'the lack of even a flimsy reason for that, justifies the understanding that the campaign is driven by an evil coven'. Hmm!! an explanation for the unfanthomed.

In a closing brief glimpse on the past for this: - The German Writer, Thomas Mann (1875-1955) stated that 'man is a master of contradictions, they exist through him and so he is grounder than they'. Without getting deep into any form of comparative (based on times and places) analysis, it is obvious these contradictions still exists through us but we may hardly any-longer be fit to be classed as masters; since the reach onto their control has eluded us.

-       The more modern opinion of USA Writer, F Scott Fitzgerald (1896-1940) that 'the test of a first-rate intelligence is the ability to hold two opposed ideas in mind at the same time and still retain the ability to function'; is surely fanciful and apparently eulogizes the ability and deeds of some of us. However, the current knowledge that intelligence testing is subject to purposes, leaves the relevance subjective.

-       The less than half century opinion of French Philosopher, Maurice Merlear Pouty (1908-1961) that 'the sane man is not one who has eliminated all contradictions from himself so much as the one who uses contradictions and involves them in his work', rather does leave much 'food for thoughts' for us to be empathetic on the present loves for chaotic contradictions.

Antagonism is a form of struggle within a contradiction
but not the universal form.
(**Mao Zedong** 1893-1976)

E L Nwankwo (May 2013)

CHAPTER : FIVE

A man should never be ashamed to own
he has been in the wrong which is but saying,
in other words, that he is wiser today than he was yesterday.
-**Alexander Pope**-(1688-1744)

THE WISDOM OF Ben Ali

The understanding that history ultimately judges events, actions and even circumstances; has mostly presupposed that a hundred or when rather quick fifteen to twenty years would elapse for such to crystalize. The present generation has been much described in a variety of impatient and quick service terms. Most of which harbour more negative connotations than anything worthy. The phenomenal spread of 'microwave' attitude seems to have infectiously afflicted today's history, on a minor aspect of the catastrophic events of the Arab Spring. More than twenty two months after the Arab Spring demonstrations started; outside that narrow region and apart from those following the unfolding tragedy, not many in Europe, Asia, the Americas and even Africa, would now (in Oct 2012) remember the name: Ben Ali.

A little more than few may outside the Muslim areas still recall that Tunisia is the cradle of the Arab Spring. Ben Ali was that nation's Head of State when the demonstrations erupted. Tunisia is neither a major oil exporter nor does it have a history of recent international political activism. It neither lies in any 'indulgent materials' trade route nor its tourism potential with a backing of its citizens having a servitude attitude in the quest of foreign currency. Added to all those; for all that Ben Ali could have been, unlike some heads of state on the international scene, he appeared not to be a showman of a noteworthy category. Not, a fiery orator like Chavez, nor adventurous like Sarkozy, forceful like Gaddafi, charming like Bill Clinton, stunt loving like Putin or assertive like G W Bush. He was however in the elite and exclusive league of dictator leaders in office for over twenty years without succession or retirement plans. Emperors, who actually; deceitfully instigate being referred to, as President.

By nature's unchangeable circumstance, all leaders eventually get removed from office. So, prime ministers, presidents, imperial leaders and emperors alike, go by design or ousted by acts of nature. The regrettably very costly oustings within the Arab Spring events, are definitely not fair to be classed as nature designed exists for those helmsmen but more so, for their nations. Nature plays no part in any case of systematic attempt of extermination by one, of his own people. Rather this regional spectre of violence fully fits into the Sigmund Freud and co theory on violence being inherent in man; with the support slant of the biological perspective from hereditary and behavioral studies that: man is particularly aggressive and has an unequalled lust to kill his like. That is only to highlight but not to justify nor rationalize on a heinous historical penchant.

Principally; coup d'état, death and abdication are the conventional means by which totalitarian rulers exit the scene. Most get into office by machevialian means of subtle or brazen inducement of any of the above three means on their predecessors. In life, obviously like begets like, with an attendant likelihood of escalation of unchecked evil as mantle of leadership passes. In the case of Ben Ali, his exit though unconventional, properly fits into the abdication category. An act or situation, more for this purpose implies a formal relinquishing or giving up of sovereign power with no option of a reclaim. In this case, it was prompted by the massive and widespread civil unrest that broke out on or about 23rd Dec 2010 following the suicide of 26year old Mohammed Bouazizi (a jobless graduate who burnt himself to death because police confiscated his fruit cart). The destructive unrest continued for days, peaking after Friday Muslim prayers. The response of the military and police, with excessive force; to demonstrate the authority of their leader (who was in his 23rd year in office), resulted in a few dozen deaths nationwide. Contrary to the character traits of totalitarian rulers, Zine al-Abidine Ben Ali, not many days into the mayhem viewed the carnage, resilience and trend; suddenly quit and promptly fled to Saudi Arabia on 14th Jan 2011. Thus a mix of purely domestic implosive forces had catalyzed a modern abdication. A real and irreversible exit of a ruler; not the comic events where some 'step aside' but continue to pull all the strings behind closed public doors.

Like a wildfire; copy-cat demonstrations broke-out in also restive neighboring Middle- East (Muslim) nations also saddled with similar veteran totalitarian rulers. Particular mention has to be made of Col Gaddafi of Libya and Hosni Mubarak of Egypt, because both men publicly mocked Ben Ali after news of his self-exile to Saudi broke-out. It is flabbergasting that both being more of veteran despots should so do. No reports yet indicate that their aides reminded them that 'those who live in glass houses ought not to throw stones'.

With a central issue of this matter (abdication) broached, a cursory look at very few historic examples maybe worthy. The choice nominees would include Nebuchadnezzar from the book of Daniel in the Holy Bible and Napoleon I both of whom are many times over more prominent and or notorious than Ben Ali. Arrogance was a common character feature of both. The first was divinely cast out, for a seven year sojourn in the wilderness, to be on the same pedestal with beasts. Austria, Russia, Prussia and Britain by the 1814 Treaty of Chaumonth united to force out Napoleon; who was eventually exiled to the Island of Elba. The intriguing plots and maneuvers of Napoleon's ousting remains a tutoring example for diplomacy in some circles.

The spread of the escalating Muslim Arab violent civil unrests next became prominent in Egypt; where nemesis (without any obvious contributions of the long subdued opposition- Moslem Brotherhood) caught-up with Hosni Mubarak. After several weeks of riotous destructions and a few hundred deaths, he was ousted by his military high command. As he failed to flee, after a year of judicial trial, he was 'mercifully' jailed for life. Meanwhile, a member of the Moslem Brotherhood had won the election and was sworn-in as President. As for the now late Col M Gaddafi; in his mindlessly brutal quest, to completely crush all protests within Libya, his elite forces along with his paid mercenaries committed what ought to be classed as pogrom in Ziltan and Misrata. With a UN imposed no-flights over the nation's airspace, NATO's support bombing raids of his military machinery enabled the rebelling massive popular opposition to overcome, capture and kill him on 21st Oct 2011. Many months after the uprising erupted, the ethnic biased massacre by Gaddafi left echoing disenchantments and recurring retaliatory armed violence in Libya late into year 2012.

Thereafter, the prime theater of the Arab Spring violence shifted to Yemen. Here again was another veteran, arrogant and particularly sly despot. Sly, because time after another, he demonstrated what Niccol Machiavelli in the book 'The Prince' suggested that, 'a prudent ruler ought not to keep faith when by so doing it would be against his interest. ..Nor have legitimate grounds ever failed a prince who wished to show colorable excuse for the nonfulfillment of his promise'. Again but after many months of killings and wanton destruction, Saleh, the President (who was later during the unrests, hospitalized in Saudi Arabia for mortar attack injuries) was eventually diplomatically induced and eased out of power by a coalition of Arab and Western nations led by Saudi Arabia. Another case, of induced abdication and exile to Saudi Arabia. Meanwhile, within all the theaters of the uprisings, theories have been put forward as to the factors that, to some extent prolong the resistance to the civil unrests. They mainly include but are not limited to: ethnic diversity of the nations, terrain, national wealth/petroleum, foreign influence, neighbors, foreign relations and the personality of the head of state. All or most of which seem to relevantly contribute to the now (Oct 2012) much prolonged (i.e.: having lasted 19months with a death-toll in excess of 32,000) dire situation in Syria. In this nation, Bashar al Assad the head of state (a Surgeon by Profession) at the age of 47, is continuing a (40year old, i.e., after his dad) brutal family leadership dynasty. Like the Gaddafi ruining of Misrata, al Assad has laid large areas of the city of Homs waste.

So in retrospect, looking at the collateral damages, human and economic losses that those nations have sustained just for the bizarre excuse of one man continuing in an office he had over used, abused and not served for decades; simply makes the description - absurd; much inadequate. On that basis, it can be suggested that, be it inadvertently, unwittingly or whatever; the rather quick abdication of Ben Ali, grossly saved his nation Tunisia the likes of historical losses and trauma that Libya and Syria may take dozens of years to recover from. Which brings to reckon, the saying by French Philosopher Rene Descartes that, 'it is not enough to have a good mind but the main thing is to use it well'. In those circumstances, there is not a tinge but a lot of commendable comparable wisdom in the timing of Zine al-Abidine Ben Ali's abdication.

E L Nwankwo (Oct 2012)

PART B

CHAPTER: SIX

The sublime and the ridiculous are often so
related that it is difficult to class them separately.
-**Thomas Paine**-*(1737-1809)*

THE SEASIDE LURE

Fantasy naturally covets no better locale than the likes of seasides. To the sublime, his day of concerns is therein blessed by no advanced notice for the soothing. To the clairvoyant, this his choice trade precinct maintains an unknown day of reckoning. To the Casanova, his sessions of elation near those, never escape sobering reality. To the inexperienced passerby, the seductive aura beside such is not short of a phantom. Also, to the farmer, fisherman and mariner whose jobs there depends, Mother Nature's necessity packages a familiar yet occasionally strange swathes.

The poetic and panoramic head-start in even content and context ought not to becloud this: a brief, taking issues with some 'seaside' matters of our times. If we briefly cast our attention back to historical accounts in the scriptures, we affirm that the lure to seasides; service different purposes. At a cliff type, demons allowed into a herd of swine by Jesus perished into the sea below. (a case of riding the area of 'waste'). For the beach type, on more than one occasion He (Jesus Christ) used the meeting to teach and miraculously feed thousands of those present. Earlier, prominent disciples of His had been recruited from the seashores. So in multiple styles and state, our factors of nature meet in fashions that bemuse the littleness of man. Where the tidally rising and ebbing, yet never drying oceans meet the firmament, scenic domains emerge. Where rock outcrops intervene, precipitous cliffs in awe eliminate shared pathways. Otherwise, at the other end of circumstances the twice daily 'washing' of the sand, by tides levels and cleans the grounds. In this later case, when wide enough, a seaside beach beckons unto all, not just to the melancholic. In the midst of the wide divide of both, are the less majestic types of forest low banked mangroves and salt-marshes which are often thickly vegetated to impede access (usually more in the tropics). Yet, these with unchallenging topography lack scenic awesomeness. It's loss, nature compensated with peculiar plant life and as sanctuary to a wide variety of wildlife. Therein shore-birds, sea turtles and the likes of alligators nest to hatch their young.

On the crags of the rocky cliffs, mountain goats and birds of prey establish habitations; as sand crabs and periwinkles colonize the waves swept sand beaches. For all that these splendour maybe worth, man on the guise of preserving nature in many nations designates many areas of the meeting of two 'worlds' as reserved natural parks. The fact that more often than not, portions of the reservations are made picnic areas, nature trails, avian sanctuary and even camp-grounds betrays the greater need to suit human fancy.

In effect, of the three, only the gentle sloped sand beaches and the thickly vegetated mangroves, in different perspectives hold the lure to much human admiration. Where the sand beach stretch is interspaced with sand dunes, frolicking by even vacationing children becomes a memorable and adoring pursuit into dusk. The soothing evening sea breeze in barely isolated surroundings brings out or enable the emergence of the subdued Casanova in even otherwise gentle but hot-blooded youth. Any wonder that sunset beach parties require not much alcohol for the incredulous to spread wide. The also sure seductions of the mangrove deltaic creeks, takes a different form. In these, in some areas the natural architectural layout of the meandering levee creeks and channels match the anastomosing dexterity of weaver birds' nests. Curiously also, their mosquito infestations and foul smelling shores at low tides takes nothing away from their clairvoyantly hypnotic summertime sunset scenery. Need we to add that, where found in developing nations, these precincts inspite of the fisheries resources they provide, are made receptacles of all forms of human effluents (industrial, domestic and agricultural). These low-lying coastal forms, for there picturesque, like the tropical rainforest are in progressive recession. That at the mouth of river Niger before the now undisputed threats of global warming innundations of low-lying coastal landforms, had for over thirty years been subjected to petroleum exploration and exploitation pollution stresses. So, an economic pursuit can also represent an environmentally destructive seaside financial lure.

So the aspects of lures, to our seasides is wide and transcends generational factors. However with limits to every environment's sustainability, and noticeable vegetative aberrations, it is obvious that in even certain elsewhile pristine locations a natural recovery threshold has been exceeded. If so, are aspects of our factors of lures, by our hands going the way of the dinosaurs?

E L Nwankwo (Oct 2012)

THE WAY OF THE WORLD

In spite of their attitudes and most derogatory postures painted of them; Nigerians the people at the trigger and heart of Africa, have traditional sayings that give credence to some very thought provoking statements of some yester years great men and sages. Ponder over these: "that when dogs are destined to die, they perceive not the odour of feaces". Also that; it is only the stubborn fly that follows the coffin into the grave"

For those with a good sense of history even on a limited scale or duration spanning less than a century; do relate the above, with a saying of Mahatma Gandhi on things that will destroy humanity, with regard to happenings around the world in the immediate past twenty years. The saying on wreck for humanity cautions on:

☐　Politics Without Principle

☐　Pleasure Without Conscience

☐　Knowledge Without Character

☐　Wealth Without Work

☐　Business Without Morality

☐　Science Without Humanity &

☐　Worship Without Sacrifice.

The truth of these could not have been better demonstrated from the sight of the extent and number of twisted faces among the representatives of "powerful" nations, in reaction to the suggestion of the immediate past Secretary General of UN Mr. Koffi Annan; that what constitutes any form of terrorism ought to be established universally.

As a byline; let all be reminded of what the Holy Book The Bible clearly states:

That the seed you sow

You shall surely reap.

ENYI: 050307 (0500 HRS)

CHAPTER: SEVEN

How beautiful it would be to see man wrestle with
his illusions and vanquish them.
-**Naguib Mahfouz**-(1911-2006)

SWAMPS AND CITY'S FLOODS

Swamps are ecosystems of a peculiar nature: structurally as well as in their dominant faunal and floral compositions. These absorbent environments naturally soak up precipitation runoff of surrounding higher grounds and by coincidence of adjoining human settlements serves as the receptacle of domestic and industrial wastes. These habitats are associated with both temporary and permanent water bodies; in low-lying coastal areas, as well as hinterland where geological circumstances so dispose.

Man as the earth's top and dominant operator, is inclined to serve his purposes often and wherever. So, man's penchant for modifications, to serve his purposes, has not spared swamps. Among many more, he has blasted tunnels through mountains for roads; dammed river courses for hydroelectricity and agricultural irrigation and even erected platforms offshore to drill oil and land air planes. So, swamps usually close to his residence and activity centers, tends to be more interfered with. Many mega cities of the world are within lowlands adjacent to swamps.

The modifications for expanding urbanization mostly provides for no credible or sustainable substituting means for the environments to continue to serve their natural purposes. The modifications so made, from a geomorphological point of view, are mostly superficial.

However, here the highlights is on the consequence of interfering with the capacity of swamps to absorb rain (precipitation run-off) and overflow flood waters from the upper reaches of river systems. In streetwise language, the issue is that, whenever swamps are built up without providing for its continued storage of flood waters of the surroundings, the low-lying nearby city's runoff water would not be quickly absorbed. So a flooding situation would arise, as soon as the area's drainage capacity (natural and artificial) is exceeded.

The focus of this does not include the likes of large swathes of Netherlands and or New Orleans coasts of USA, that are actually at or below sea level.

For the everyday language person, a swamp for this purpose can be likened to a sponge made of foam. When not compressed and water comes in contact with it, it absorbs much of the water rather quickly; only to later, gradually release the same. Hopefully, that highly simplified analogy, equally gives an indication as to why the fancied canals of many coastal cities that in time and circumstances prove to be inadequate; are no functional substitutes. Actually, that is because, canals by their design and nature can only channel a specific maximum volume of water (based on its construction configurations) to a form of downstream receptacle. Whereas most swamps feature some form of swallower network of inter connected and meandering canals (which aids fast evaporation); while the underlying peculiar soil structure, allows for massive and quick soak up (like foam) of the flood water. The later drainage of the soaked waters, unlike its absorption is gradual. In effect, most current concrete canal designs, vastly reduces the second and shuts-out the third functions (i.e. evaporation and absorption) of swamps on runoff (flood) water.

Without giving the impression of offering excuses for the bad manners of most urban high density city dwellers (within developing and third world nations alike), who inappropriately dump domestic wastes into storm drains (especially while it is raining), thereby aiding an easy clogging of the systems; rather city and state officials ought to come to terms with the fact. That is that, the design of most of their drainage systems is both inappropriate and inadequate; but they rather solely blame the failure on clogging by the bad habit and practice of their urban slum citizens. Of more concern and added to the above; is the fact of United Nations (UN) sponsored environmental research (on weather and climatic matters) that indicates that the recent escalation in floodings in populated low-lying areas may not soon abate, because of the unlikely reversal of climate change events triggered by features of global warning. It is further discomforting but necessary to mention that a Reuters news agency quoted report by the International Global Re-insurance Company, Munich Re (also of March, 2012), indicates that since 1980 globally, there has been a three-fold rise in weather related natural disasters, mostly as windstorms and floodings. The said bleak report update of March, 2012 by UN Climate Panel, indicates that these extreme weather events are likely to increase in frequency, intensity and even in extent. It was however concluded with a passionate plea: that a quick and strong political will is needed to undertake measures to protect all who maybe in the pathway of those manifestations.

Granted that in Nigeria, the governmental agency NDDC and few other companies have undertaken shoreline protection projects; it is hoped that mangrove re-vegetation projects that are ongoing be strictly seen as environmental resuscitation activities. Not part of medium and or long term measures to help protect those exposed along the pathways of rising ocean levels and extreme weather events.

As ought to be obvious, flooding is only one of the issues, the said report highlights. An event like the mid-March, 2012 unusual dense dust cloud; that covered the airspace of Yola (North-East Nigeria), with the result that commercial flights therein were cancelled for days; is an example. Also the extensive local recent changed rains pattern and areas of intensity shifts (to which we may to some extent attribute the August, 2011 flooding of parts of Ibadan: not precisely the governments recently dyked Ogunkpa rivers area that rendered about 1500 homeless and drowned approximately 100 persons); ought to finally erase any leftover iota of imagination of our location being immune from those else-while weather aberrations.

Unfortunately, current trends so point to a likely increase in city's flooding incidents. It is so noteworthy to restate that drainage designs that failed to properly take into account the geomorphology of its locality and the area's 15 year historical flood regime; as well as occluded the adjoining surfaces for quick subterranean flood waters absorption, would in a short time prove to be flawed and ineffective

E. L. NWANKWO (JUNE 2012)

WHEN A MAN IS DYING

1.   *When most things do not matter much any more*
      Frustrations are compounded by despair
      When even dreams last so consciously long:
      Then a man is dying.

2.   *When past achievements seem a colossal waste*
      Familiar disappointments are laced with deceit
      When simple human judgment is blurred by emotional
      Boredom
      Then a man is dying.

3.   *When redundancy sets in prior to any period of work*
      Desperate irrational and baseless thoughts flash
      Through the mind
      When even water seems to cause constipation
      Then a man is dying.

4.   *When lavish faultfinding becomes a pleasurable past time*
      the difference between good and bad becomes hazy
      When even the ability to trust and hope vanishes
      Then a man is dying.

ENYI-090786 (23.45HRS)

CHAPTER : EIGHT

The fact that an opinion has been
widely held is no evidence that it
is not utterly absurd.
-**Bertrand Russell**-(1872-1970)

FUNNY NATURE FROM ECOLOGY: 1
[The Big Cats]

The strategic economy of group hunting by spotted hyenas and the swift lone-ranging predation by leopards, earn them apex placements in Biologists' food chains. Some however say that for baseline reality, that amounts more to paper accolade.

Take a panoramic trip to the fringes of the Serengetti in East Africa, when rain fails and draught cakes the soil of the plains, dehydration tasks body water conservation; shortly after, the spectacular migratory trek kicks-off. This part of the story is not on the trek but on the assumed rulers of the plains, whose cousin, the lion is prided as king of the forests.

These man christened 'rulers' of those niches of the wild are actually only predatory specialists. Often they are unable to reside in different kinds of shelter or survive on a variety of food types. To crown their poorly mentioned adaptive qualities, nature bestowed them with relatively less efficient water retention abilities. Even after birth, their young are helpless and take longer to wean. As the story similarly replicates in the different environments of abode of these hunter king types; any wonder that poaching in game reserves is merely adding to their extinction stress? Which probably is contributed more to, by distorted and extended periods of draught linked to the weather aberrations of global warming.

If this light-hearted issue, is all a joke, ask paleontologists to give acceptable reasons why the enduring claim that the carnivorous dinosaurs first became extinct?

This reasoning lends some weight as to why the big cats of the wild are much represented on the endangered species lists. So, though nature made these kings of the wild hunting machines, the necessity of balance left them striped of some essential adaptation attributes. As such, man's arrogation of kingship maybe is from his usual storehouse of mockery, not nature's endowment.

So, are you a human habit replica of the big cats? If probable, your serious concerns of ever being chased off your kills by the increasing number of ferocious scavenger packs [a thoughts provoking scenario of the wild, championed by hyenas]; though genuine, is less of a threat to your survival than the consequences of your inability to adapt to your changing environment. If you doubt me, look around European politicians (of year 2012) who were dictating harsh austerity measures and preaching of the cosmic wisdom of International Monetary Fund (IMF) to their constituents.

Without shedding a tear for any, again a panoramic viewing of some Pacific and Atlantic islands without the big cats, still present picturesque sceneries of balanced ecosystems. So, without the substandard resort to excuses; please avoid questioning nature.

E L Nwankwo [May 2012]

FUNNY NATURE FROM ECOLOGY: 2

[Termite Colonies]

The endowment of ability to live within and exploit a variety of different environment types is not exclusive to man. His earlier occastrated (but now waned) attempts to expand such to the moon, uninhabited planet Mars and even choice deep ocean locations; not-withstanding. The hype having been dipped by both no longer robust economy and exploratory expedition results far short of expectations as well as lacking economic viability. Comparatively, the prudence of termite species and subspecies thus highlights nature's unequivocal balance.

Without boring most with their entomological details, many are conversant with three 'clans' of termites. First, those more easily seen within tropical forests and woodlands; where they erect conspicuous spare-shaped anthills that reach heights of two meters or more. Another's mounds are roundishly tortoise shaped and rearly exceeds a height of sixty centimeters. Lastly, those that relentlessly prefer to invade house construction timber and wooden furniture with topically encased fragile pathways and after long destructive intervals erect (i.e.: in-place of mounds), tiny nests at few timber-joints. So these poorly evolved but firmly social insects, in their diversity do not fail to fascinate even casual observers:

- For their feats, efficiency and resilience in erection of gigantic anthills that are by fair evaluations edifices.

- in some areas, though often visited by aardvarks on termite eating sprees, the undaunted worker termites steadfastly repair the break-in feeding access, while the prolific queen termite (matched by no other insect queen) lays up-to thirty five thousand eggs daily to replace the lost batches of worker and soldier termites.

- some types in the tropics with extensive chambers in large anthills may harbor birds, lizards, snakes, beetles or millipedes; in certain unobstructed parts. - their natural ability to migrate underground coupled with rapid reproduction has enabled them not being reduced to endangered species listing, let alone extermination by man during his era of lavish use of DDT (chemical pesticide) for pests control.

Mention of DDT presupposes that, that 'chemical weapon's' attack is all man has for termites. Surely, no!! In tropical Africa, eastern Nigeria to be precise, two edible species are joyously gathered by children during their seasonal nuptial flights for roasting before use as snacks. Not baffling but thought-provokingly funny that man in political arena these days can be electorally punished for double speaking, principally because of his lust for aggression when in power; but as biological scientists, he says that termites are poorly evolved (citing his rating of structural features) and in narrating their habits, is emphatic that they are much socially organized. Infact, as well as bees and not matched by any other living things. This same man in his proclaimed cradle of civilization (though many jump to deny it) was smart to adapt the internal design features of termite anthills to the final resting domain of their revered kings. The pyramids were the mummified Pharaohs of Egypt 'slept' in death.

So again another trite; yet significant and enduring exhibition of nature's, maybe clairvoyant supremacy over man. Yes they are fragile forms; do habit various places; so much of a wood destructive pest; few of which happen to be a delicacy to some and endowed with a cute prolific reproductive ability to shove aside decades of extermination attempts. Termites: another gimmick on man courtesy of nature.

E L Nwankwo (Sept 2012)

FUNNY NATURE FROM ECOLOGY: 3

[Animal flights]

Some now say that 'when dry bones are mentioned, older women make uneasy shifts'. But their flesh loving nieces and daughters promptly mutter thanks to GOD, as the ones easy for them to remember are the discarded 'drum sticks' of the flightless birds (chicken) they consume lavishly. Yes, at least for that they acknowledge God's provisional wisdom of the easily domesticated, reproductively prolific and quick growing resource. Infact over a hundred million are daily killed to meet the worldwide human carnivorous lust. However, that irreversible and pitiable avian plight is not the thrust of this time on flight.

Actually, when animal flight is botched as a topic, the thought of birds takes the central stage. While only fisheries ecologists may remember a smallish tropical fresh back-water fish like Pantodon bucholzii that takes to brief aerial jump glidings; many more who are observant at dusk, point also to bats. Only a fraction of whom know that those bats are mammals; be they fruits or insects eating types. Their few blood sucking (vampire) types get much more mention than their activities, population size and habitat extent. So, while only birds and bats can flap to fly, all other animals involved with flights can only glide. So they basically hop-off from a point, promptly spread-out their parachuting membranes and glide to a lower point or to the ground.

Man, the so endowed but surely copy-cat specialist has in a myriad of adaptations put all flight forms to use. In pursuit of fun and sport, gliding is an all-seasons activity. His ingenuity let him reorient flapping wings (which he could not efficiently mechanically device), unto rotating propellers that also provided the thrust for a lift. Having achieved flight capability, trust nature's only lustfully aggressive primate; fun, sport and commerce shortly after only constituted secondary concerns for the use of being airborne. In-case you do not already get the picture; by the onset of second world war (WW-II) when the feat of mass production of light aircrafts had been mastered, both the Nazis and the allied nations spent material, human and financial fortunes to produce the 'toys' for massive killing and destructions. It is only the naive that would imagine that the urge or penchant to adaptively improve on those flight killing machines cooled off with that war. Today (like in Syria, in that nation's 'Arab spring' mayhem) flight machines that are fast, can fly low and remain flying on a spot, as humming birds do (we refer to helicopters) are used by some leaders to kill their nation's citizens (compatriots). Stealth crafts (dedicated purely for aggressive military purposes) are in operation which fly high, fast, for long and highly evasively; a combined adaptations of the habits and qualities of kites, some migratory birds and bats. Even unmanned and remote controlled missiles firing drones are in violent use in parts of Afghanistan. Other complimenting features of those flight animals like visual acuity, echo-location and night vision have all also in various modes been adapted for operational effectiveness of those war crafts.

So while the copy-cat syndrome unabated flourishes, we can in defense of man point-out that in the wild while the reptile chameleon and a fish (like the parasitic Blenny that fakes as a cleaner-fish to approach the much larger Snapper) use similar maneuvers (referred to as mimicry by biologists) for defensive camouflage and hunting; even some types of pitcher plants do the like to capture insects which they digest. Those however neither justifies nor explains the depths of man's lust for unprovoked aggressions more so in use of adaptations from nature that ought to impact more positively.

E L Nwankwo (Sept 2012)

FUNNY NATURE FROM ECOLOGY 4

(Seasonal Migrations)

The mention of seasonal migrations to most swings the mind to the local more prominent or spectacular exodus or influx of populations at specific periods of the year. The purposes being, to seek refuge from the ravages of nature (weather) and recourse to an area more suitable for reproductive perpetuation of the species. A few widely known examples would do for this purpose:

(A)   Though the East-African wild animals' Serengeti trek involves multiple species, groups of such stay together within the pack.

(B)   The cross-continental multitudes of bird's migrations from temperate zones to the tropics during winter

(C)   The annual reproductory migration of the Atlantic Eel (a serpentine fish) from the equatorial Sargasso Sea of Central America, into West European fresh water rivers to further grow after spawning.

Man's seasonal vacationing movements in some localities doesn't fit or purposefully replicate guiding principles and factors of the above listed examples; as the choice destinations are strictly more influenced by cash flow than any other factors. When a season that limits shelter and grossly reduces food availability sets-in; some wild animals (birds and mammals alike) in large single-species groups depart their primary dwellings for another. The 'refuge' locations and their access route yearly remains about the same. It is only on the occasions of reproductory migration, that only the reproducing adults of the population alone, make the trip. Which in no way ought to be likened to the honeymooning of human newly-weds or vacationing couples.

Actually, the following are few relevant basic points of note on peculiarities of migrations:

1; the same migration route is used yearly by birds and animals.

2; the choice destination remains for reproductive trips and varies insignificantly for entire populations escaping a local harsh (weather) period.

3; both differ from man's motives for change of environment. Which mainly are for:

[a]- Recreational pleasure

[b]- moving away from areas of famine and conflicts (war zones).

4; And man's occasions are not for specific yearly periods.

5; unlike man that often induces refugeeing population drifts by sieges and wars, no incident of animal or birds migration has ever occurred or been recorded, as being on account of non-human predatory stress.

Again checkered, skewed, distorted and misapplied adaptations from nature by us (man). Funny, nutty and cheeky *homo sapiens sapiens* (n/b: don't forget, that's man's biological name); but more for this purpose: 'a twisting copy-cat'.

E L Nwankwo (Feb 2013)

CHAPTER: NINE

Who has seen the wind? Neither you
nor I, but when the trees bow down
their heads; The Wind is passing by
*-**Christiana Rossetti**-(1830-1894)*

AN EPOCH OF NATURAL DISASTERS

In an earlier write-up on Emergency Response (i.e.; the third of a three part presentation), with a subtitle of "the changing outlook of natural disasters", a brief was given on a select few of natural disasters that occurred between April, 2010-Jan, 2011. There, the emphasis was justification for planning for natural disasters; the needs for such, in both cosmopolitan and industrial settings, being the basis. However, the focus of this seeming sequel to "the changing outlook of natural disasters" is rather to raise awareness to a possible onset of distinctive and significant developments worldwide. In the said previous presentation, mention was made of currently and apparently disproportionately higher spate of natural disasters, with elevated intensities as well as extents (coverage areas) being comparatively out of-scale.

From the descriptions contained in the Encarta dictionaries of 2009 on a significant time frame with reference to the occurrence of historic events; an epoch is a much shorter duration than an era. That categorization borrowed from geological classifications has not much to do with the fact that this discuss is on mainly tectonic upheavals and meteorological aberrations; but that the reference time duration is short and quite recent. Infact the type of reference called "just yesterday" in Nigerian proverbial folklore terms. Naturally, that time blurs the accuracy of recollecting past events, may additionally justify our restricting the focus period to the recent.

Natural disasters result from earthquakes, volcanic eruptions, floods, hurricanes, tornadoes and weather extremes. Those can secondarily give rise also to landslides, tsunami, blizzards, sandstorms and thunder induced forest fires. That catalogue shows the broad spectrum of sources of natural disasters. Recently however, because of the hazard potential to jet engines and extent of civil aviation flights disruptions caused by airborne drifting volcanic dust particles; that as well has become a significant secondary source.

For the short time duration between April 2010 and Jan, 2012 disasters both man-made and natural have been much reported. Though the spate, intensities and extent of both types appear higher than the events of the immediate past years; those of natural disasters are much more. In some instances they are comparatively out-of-scale with recent historic reference incidents. That is not meant to disregard the also escalated worldwide incidents of civil strife and sabotage; exemplified by the Arab Spring situations, Al Qaeda in Pakistan and Afghanistan and even the comparatively smaller scaled Boko-Haram skirmishes in Northern Nigeria. Rather than compare, the essence of this (as already hinted) is to raise awareness to a possible on-set of distinctive and significant developments worldwide.

These natural disasters of seismic and meteorological origin within the discuss period (mainly of April 2010- Jan 2012) have been devastating on account of many factors.

However, the central issue of this lighthearted panoramic overview has to do with, if there is even a remote likelihood that the said factors of the manifestations could result to significant changes. Even if changes of restoring the long 'man-distorted' environmental (ecosystematic) equilibrium (from the global warming perspective), added to a probable nature's gradual re-equilibration of the system (which includes tectonic adjustments in the form of upheavals). This picture scope so, includes the current contributions of tectonic activities along with the primarily weather and climate change focus of global warming. Highlights on some (focused on earthquakes, volcanic eruptions, floodings/tsunamis and weather extremes/aberrations) may suffice:

EARTHHQUAKES:

While to most of us laymen; earthquakes (also referred to as: tremor or quakes): are localized energetic and wavelike ground shaking phenomenon arising from deep underground; the relevant professionals simply describe it as: a sudden release of energy in the earth's crust that creates seismic waves. The magnitude (also known as Richter) is it's common scale of measurement. Depending on the circumstances and place, quakes can give rise to secondary disaster phenomenon such as: landslides, avalanches, ground rupture, soil liquefaction and floods. They also can trigger volcanic activities and tsunamis. The point on the earth's surface directly above the quakes origin, is referred to as its epicenter. The relationship in origin of quakes and volcanic eruptions, according to geologists, is easily seen from the mapped global earthquake epicenters and plate tectonics. As simply expected, the higher the magnitude of a quake, the higher also, its' potential for destruction.

See Table 1.

TABLE: 1- RICHTER SCALE OF QUAKE MAGNITUDE

MAGNITUDE LEVEL	CATEGORY	EFFECTS	APPROX YEARLY FREQUENCY
<1.0-2.99	Micro	Generally not felt by people	>100,000
3.0-3.9	Minor	Felt by people but no damage	12,000-100,000
4.0-4.9	Light	Felt by all; Minor breakages	2,000-12000
5.0-5.9	Moderate	Some damage to weak structures	200 – 2000
6.0 – 6.9	Strong	Moderate damage	20 – 200
7.0 – 7.9	Major	Serious damage over some area and loss of life	3 – 20
8.0>	Great	Severe destruction and loss of life over large areas	<3

As is evident from the Richter's scale, associated factors include: extent (i.e.: area subjected to the manifestation) and the estimated global annual frequency of occurrence. Both are focal reference issues of this opinion on the different aspects of natural disasters. An isolated comparative review of the New Zealand Christchurch incidents (i.e. of 7.1 mag in Sept, 2010 and 6.3 mag on Feb 21,2011) and the May,2012 Northern Italian areas of Bologna and Romagna (i.e. on 19th May: 5.9 mag and then on 29th May: 5.8mag respectively) with the standards of Richter's scale could lend some credence to a probable shift from historic pattern of events or records. For both places, the repeat events could not have been among the aftershocks. The New Zealand cases were five months apart; while the Italian cases were 10 days apart. The Sept. 2012 event though of a major category had no initial causality report. As at 21st Feb. 2011 however the initial body count (fatality) for the "follow ups" incident was 65 (n/b: it later rose to nearly 200) for a 6.3mag (strong: category) quake: which is not expected to involve loss of life. The explanation was that the structures too easily collapsed because they had been much compromised by the Mag. 7.1 Sept. 2010 event. It is doubtful, if the same reasoning path would satisfactorily explain the Italian event death toll of 3 and 17, for purely Moderate category (Mag. 5.9 and 5.8) incidents. However also, that the death toll at the Christchurch incident rose; can be associated with the added hindrances that the rescue operations encountered. As the city is built on sand and much silty soil, with a low water table (as a result of which, the quake induced soil liquefaction into mud with flooding) thus adversely hindering facets of the rescue operations. All that is added to the fact that the area sits between pacific and Indo-Australian tectonic plates; as such records about 14000 quakes yearly with about 20 of which measuring up to 5.0 on the Richter's scale.

TABLE: 2 (A) QUAKES OF LATE MAY, 2012 (14TH- 29TH)

DATE	MAGNITUDE	LOCATION	REMARKS
14TH	6.2	Peru/Chile boarder	No reported damage
18th	4.8	Eastern Japan	Rattled windows
19th	5.9	Bologna (N. Italy)	-
21st	5.6	Sofia, Bulgaria	Chimney Collapse Mini Injuries
25th	5.2	Christchurch New Zealand	No reported casualty
28th	6.4	Northern Argentina	-
29th	5.8	Romagno (N. Italy)	Extensive building Collapse. 17 dead.

(B) RECENT GREAT QUAKES (>8.0mag)

Feb. 27th 2010	8.8	Chile	Caused tsunami >500 dead, property damage $30 Billion.
March 11th 2011	9.0	Japan	Large transnational tsunami; killed> 15,000
April 11th 2012	8.6	Indonesia (Aceh)	Horizontal shift quake so did not displace enough water to trigger tsunami

Compiled from: Reuters.com web reports

From the Richter's scales, quake incidents of 6.0mag and above annually worldwide, is estimated to range from 20   200. Mathematically therefore, for a month, under 2 of such are expected. However from the tabulated incidents (please see Table 2), within the later 15days of May, 2012 three quakes of 5.9 6.4 were recorded. Also, the Great quakes (i.e. of >8.0mag) are expected to occur less than 3 times in a year (i.e. within 12 calendar months): but within 14 months (i.e.: between Feb. 27th 2010 and April 11th 2012), three of such claimed about 16,000 lives and caused property damage in excess of $100 billion.

VOLCANIC ERUPTIONS:

Due to their common origin, similar areas of prevalence and overlapping aftermath, it is easy to state the general linkage of earthquakes to volcanic eruptions. Both are natural disasters prime tectonic upheavals. Though Seismologists variedly classify volcanic activities; the spectacular explosive effusions are the commonly known. The immediate noticeable ground hazards associated with this phenomenon will include: hot lava flow, toxic gas clouds, ash/debris falls, avalanches, mud flows and tsunami. Beyond that list of eruptions' potential effects, the emission of dust clouds high into the atmosphere are equally hazardous to jet engines flights operations, as well as the reduction of visibility and weather alterations. Comparatively volcanic eruptions occur less suddenly than major quakes; as such they are much better forecast. That situation gives relatively ample time for the evacuation of people. That is simply because, they show detectable pre-eruption increasing activity; such as quakes magnitude/frequency, summit dome or fissure site deformation e.g. bulging; as well as steam/fumes effusions via vents   However, on occasions they have constituted extensive and prolonged hazards; by their extensive drifting ash/dust clouds and long duration eruptions. (E.g. in 1989, Chile's volcanic Mt. Longnimay's eruption lasted for about two months). Table 3, shows sample of peculiar events' types of eruptions' disaster factors. Those have made them historically also devastating.

TABLE 3

SOME VOLCANIC ACTIVITY TYPES

MATERIALS/ EFFECT	BRIEF ON EVENT
a) Ash dust	- Mt. Vesuvius (Southern Italy) AD 79 Eruption buried 3 cities with their Populations in ash and mudflow
b) Ash debris (rock fragments)	- Mt. Tambora (Indonesia) April 1815 eruption covered 500,000sq km with 1cm thick ash layer. Approx 1, 400m of its summit cone was blown off.
c) Tsunami	- Mt. Krakatoa (Indonesia) Aug. 1883 Eruption reduced the 450m peak to 275m below water; triggered a tsunami that killed 36,000 persons.
d) Pyroclastic Magma	- Mt. Pelee (Caribbean Sea) May, 1902 Eruption burnt to death 29,000 people with its pyroclastic magma.
e) Mud flow	- Mt. Ruiz (Andes Mountains, Columbia) Nov1985 eruption triggered mud flow that killed 22,000 persons in the town of Armero.
f) Toxic Gas	The Volcanic crater lake water column Inversion, in Aug. 1986 (i.e. lake Nyos,Camerouns), released trapped toxic gases (maybe H2S, CO etc) to the surroundings, down the slope, thus killing over 1,700.
g) Ash Clouds	- Examples of this modern-day bane of jet air travel abounds. Mt. Eyjatjallajokull (Iceland) eruption of April 2010, sent disruptive ash clouds that led to about 100,000 flights cancellations (affecting 10 million people) at about $1.7 billion costs.

Derived from Ecyclopaedia Britanica, 2010 and Encanta Dictionaries, 2009 t has been better established from satellite imaging, that most volcanic chains are located within areas of tectonic activity. Indonesia with the world's largest number of potentially active volcanoes, is within the so called tectonic "Ring of fire". Chile in South America (has a 500 chain of volcanic mountains; out of which 50 are known to have erupted) and Iceland, near the North Pole; are mapped within areas of the Plate Tectonics concept. It is therefore worthy to mention that even outside the areas of the concept, volcanic activity does occur: as was the minor Nov. 2010 case in Benue State (Nigeria) within the fringes of Cameroun mountains range; following a string of minor tremors, magma spewed from six fissures on a mountain slope. Also on Aug. 25th, 2011 in the mining district of Ariit (Niger Republic) volcanic smoke and fumes spewed for two days from a fissure on a mountain.

Beyond the list of volcanic hazards, their potential for devastation is influenced by issues like: nearness of human habitations, origin, magnitude, timing, coverage and duration. Even the nature of human activity may aid the degree of influence. So, it is arguable that flights disruptions by volcanic dust clouds of recent is prevalent because turbine jet engines which is in vogue, are susceptible to ash particles while the earlier generation propeller planes (which operate at much lower altitudes below those about which the ash clouds more often gather) are not affected to similar extents.

TABLE 4: SOME ERUPTIONS

a) RELEVANT 2010/2011 CASES

DATE	LOCATION	ACTIVITY BRIEF
April, 2010	Mt. Eyjafjallayokull (Iceland)	This glacial eruption threw dense fine particulate ash into most of the European airspace. Disrupted flights for weeks, with a 6-day complete shutdown. The 100,000 flight cancellations cost 1.7 billion dollars and affected 10m persons
Oct. 25th, 2010	Mt. Merapi (Indonesia)	Erupted twice within a week. initially triggered by a 7.5mag Quake on 24th. Killed 34 and another 343 by the tsunami it triggered.
May 21st 2011	Mt. Grimsvotn (Iceland)	This eruption from under glacier spewed a 25km high ash column Due to the heavy ash particle size spat out, flights disruptions through that route was not extensive and long. (only about 500 flights were cancelled.
June 4th, 2011	Mt. P-Gordon Caulle (Chile)	Spewed ash tower that disrupted flights in Argentina and Uruguay.
June 14th 2011	(Eritrea)	Belched ash for three days that flights in NE Africa towards Saudi Arabia. (ie; Mt Nabro) were disrupted.
(b) MAY 2012 CASES]		
02nd	Mt. Lokon (Indonesia)	Eruption at 11.55am local time.
25th	Mt. Popcatepeti (Mexico)	800m high fume emission; fragments ejection and quakes
25th	Mt. Kilauea (Hawaii, USA)	12 quakes on 24th and lava flow onto dome side.
25th	Mt. Ijen (Indonesia)	Tremors from April till 13th May
25th	Mt. Fuego (Guatemala)	Explosions and 700m high ash Column on 23rd; shock waves.
25th	Mt. Sirung. (Indonesia)	Small 3hr. ash emission on 8th May. Sulphur detected 3km North of Crater on 12th May.
25th	Mt. Santa Maria (Guatemala)	Explosions and 800m high ash column on 23rd &

Compiled from Reuters.com web reports

Table 4: on volcanic eruptions, is to give this phenomenon's replicate examples to those of quakes, in table 2. Similarly on reported incidents, their scales of influence on mankind etc., and the likely subtle shifts in pattern, are not without those who justly require more indicator references. Some of the opinions with reservations on the weighting of these change contributing factors, point to a fact that recent drifts of high population centers towards the predisposed areas aids elevated fatalities. Just like the greater dependence on turbine jet engine flights (rather than propeller planes), that would be grounded (to avoid a disastrous risk of flying as their normal cruising height approximates to 30,000ft which is well within the 20,000 35,000ft where the lighter volcanic ash particles clouds drifts). The same line of thought also cite the information technology aided ease of news gathering and disseminations as likely reason for an apparent increase in incidence frequency.

The extent (coverage area) and the duration (the period the situation lasts) of some of disaster situations (like the Nov. 2010 Jan 2011 flooding of Queensland, Australia, which was not occasioned by a hurricane like the category 5 Katrina of 2005 in New Orleans, USA), set-aside the near permissive opinions.

FLOODING/TSUNAMI

An overflow of an expanse of water that submerges land: is a simple description of flood. The year 2010 Encyclopedia Britannica defines it as: a high water stage where it overflows it's natural or artificial banks onto a normally dry land. An expansion of the Red Cross listing of the causes of flooding would include: heavy and steady rainfall over a brief period; storm surges of coastal areas and tsunamis. Flash floods and storm surges are two known but non-typical forms of floods (which are also devastating). Flash floods are sudden large volumes of torrential muddy turbulent water that rushes down a pathway. They result from summer thunderstorms or rapidly melted snow or ice. While storm surges are coastal flooding caused by a wall of water triggered from off-shore by hurricane force winds.

So the typical floods are those land inundations occasioned by excessive rainfall or the overflow of river banks (also as a result of heavy rains along the river's catchment area and upper reaches).

Another spectacular form of catastrophic flood event is the tsunami. Simply, these are ocean waves that washes ashore, having been generated or triggered by a sudden displacement of a huge volume of sea water by an earthquake, volcanic eruption or mudslide/avalanche. They are particularly devastating because their fast water walls can come ashore at heights of up-to 30m.

The above background explains why coastal cities and low lying areas adjacent to large water bodies and rivers courses are more predisposed to flooding. However, flooding still typically occurs in other places when the drainage (natural and or artificial) capacity of the area is exceeded, while water influx continues. Though there are four factors of flood measurement; only height; inundated area and the residence period (which directly reflects on scale of human suffering and devastation) are relevant to this presentation.

HIGHLIGHTS:

(A) FLOODS: Some publications including one by Red Cross stated that floods are among the most frequent and costly natural disasters. Even their death tolls exceed those of wildfires, drought and tornados. In USA, flash flood warnings in March, 2012 for Louisiana, Arkansas and Mississippi areas were repeated. The sad and tedious experience of 2010 monsoon season in Pakistan and Bangladesh is hoped not to repeat in the near future. The Nov. 2010 Jan 2011 spectacular historic flood event of the state of Queensland, Australia, remains peculiar. The said excessive rains; induced flooding that lasted several weeks. It grossly surpassed all known records for the area; on all three factors of: height (flood depth), the inundated area and the period the flood lasted. Yet contributing circumstances like the breeching of flood barriers and being triggered by hurricane force winds, as was the 2005 New Orleans Katrina; were not associated with this incident. So also are the historic case incidents of Netherlands and China; not fair to be flatly compared. In the previous, a quarter of the nation's land mass along the coasts is below sea level. Obviously the maintenance of that nation's coastal flood defense system and dykes (that in parts stretches to 100km) is a feat against the North Sea storm surges. While China's River Huang He (Yellow River) holds history's most fatal flooding record: the river's extensive silt deposition along its low-lying lower reaches, with the very heavy rains along it's catchment upper reaches; predisposes the wide lower flood plains to river course changing flood surges. Its incidents of 1931 and 1938 each inundated about 21,000 sq. km and collectively killed over two million persons.

(B) TSUNAMI: The awesome power and massive devastation potential of tsunami currently needs no emphasis. The trans-Oceanic Dec. 26th, 2004 Indian Ocean 9.1mag quake triggered incident; slaughtered all it could in its path, in more than six countries. While the mayhem and reverberations of the March 11, 2011 Fukushima, Japan 9.0mag quake induced event yet resonates. Table 5 includes three other recent incidents for mere emphasis.

RECENT TSUNAMIS

TABLE: 5

DATE/LOCATION	CAUSE	REMARK
: Dec. 26th, 2004 (Indonesia).	9.1mag Quake.	Killed about 230,000 in more than 6 countries (Indonesia, Maldives, India, Siri Lanka etc)
: July17th, 2006 (Java, Indonesia)	7.7mag Quake	Killed about 550
: Feb.27th, 2010 (Chile)	8.8mag Quake	Killed over 500
: Oct. 25th, 2010 (Indonesia)	Eruption Mt. Merapi	Eruption killed 34 Tsunami killed 343
March 11th, 2011 (Fukushima, Japan)	9.0mag Quake	Killed about 15,000

Compiled from: Reuters.com web reports.

For years; mostly the weather induced aspects of flooding have been in focus. The tectonic contributions, less retrospectively reviewed, shows that the lapse persists: because, based on the relevant aspects of their business concern, the Global Re-insurance Company, Munich Re (in a Reuters quoted report of March 2012) stated that since 1980, weather related disasters (like windstorms and floods) have more than tripled worldwide.

WEATHER EXTREMES/ABBERATIONS:

A Wikipedia encyclopedia description states that these are: weather phenomenon that are at the extremes of historical distribution; out of season and especially severe. These varied forms of weather upheavals, unlike the other factors of natural disasters: are more climate specific, in some circumstances less easily predictable and can also be dramatically brief. Some of the prominent forms would include: cold snaps, dust clouds/storms, heat waves, tropical cyclones, tornadoes, thunderstorm etc. Some listings also include significant distortion of seasonal periods and even wild fires. As a result of the large composition of this group of events, even a brief description of any would be avoided.

As has been the thrust of this presentation, an attempt is made to show or ascertain if there are recent: significant increase in the record of these events: escalation of their intensities or even an extension of their historical devastation pathways. As already mentioned in the section above on floodings; the Global re-insurance company Munich Re; in a report stated that natural disasters of this categorization (though rear as they occur only about 5% of the times) on a global level, have tripled since 1980 in recorded incident rates. Also, a publication by a group of researchers (Hoyos et al, 2006: as quoted by a Reuters.com web report) claims that the recent increase in number of category 4 and 5 hurricanes is linked to global temperature increases.

SOME AREA HIGHLIGHTS:

(a)   **USA** In 2008, nine (9) disastrous weather events (made-up of tropical cyclones, heat and cold waves) were recorded, and by 2011, the figure rose to 12. Due to distortions within the season, year 2012 winter was un-usually warm while 2011 summer was blistering. The consequence of this was that definitive snowfall failure and recurring ambient temperature swings (i.e. into the highs) was with areas like Chicago in 2012.

(b)   **EUROPE:** The devastation (with relatively few fatalities) of 2012 by drifting winter cold snaps; is the reference event here. From late January into and mid-February, the freezing cold snaps (i.e. of about 300c: a level more than 12 degrees lower than any in 50 years for most of the said localities); mostly in the Balkans killed many homeless persons. 215 in Russia, 135 in Ukraine, 86 in Romania, 45 in Italy, 32 in Bulgaria, 5 in France etc. A total of, 810.

(c) **AFRICA:** The trend having, been established for this group of natural disasters events; only two "small spots would be picked for emphasis from Africa. Yola (a lower North-East town in Nigeria). For over ten days after mid-March 2012, was un-usually covered by a dust cloud so much it disrupted commercial flights to its airport. The seasonal disruptions of 2012 also did cause a significant mid-March early rains failure in much of Uganda (especially Entebbe to Kampala Areas).

BYELINE:

The March 2012 report of United Nations (UN) Climate Panel (which agrees with most issues of climate change including the rise in Ocean levels: as such subjecting coastal dwellers worldwide to increasing frequency and levels of floodings); counsels that now, with the short term irreversible trends, political-will should be gathered to quickly protect all those in the pathways of natural disaster events.

E L Nwankwo (June 2012)

POSTSCRIPT WRAP-UP

Echo.....call her and she will call you
Curse her and she will curse you
You can not win if you argue
The last word is always hers
 -**Ai Qing**- (1910-1996)

Confusion is a word we have
invented for an order which
is not understood
        -**Henry Miller**-(1891-1980)

Pretense surely guides most evasive commentaries. Oh! Could that not be stated a little less bluntly? A counsel often given more to serve the agenda of its source. Having 'looked' through the opening chapters on 'A Way of Men' and 'Glimpse on Tyranny of Freedoms'; Francisco Margell who said 'every man who has power over another is a tyrant', the French Poet Charles P Pegny who quipped that 'tyranny is always better organized than freedom' and US Historian Hannah Arendt, that 'under conditions of tyranny, it is easier to act than think'; the perspective ought to become clear. If any doubts linger especially on the first, recall that the Russian Revolutionary Leon Trotsky once said 'an ally has to be watched just like an enemy', while George Bush (a US president) who, on a televised national address said 'a time of historic change is no time for recklessness', thereafter went to war much too quickly than expected. An adventure historically proved poorly timed and wasteful.

However, while many insist that nothing is new in this world, only a few would disagree that the present generation often comes up with new unimaginable scopes and versions of old misdemeanors. In times past some nations were held hostage by local military cliques (junta as referred to by some). Such was prevalent in Africa and the Middle-East 1970-2000. It's twin; the undemocratic one party state system of China and North Korea, remain like an un-quarried granite. But the new fledging breeds here in part focus (yet to actually run any governments) could include the likes of Columbian drug cartels and the US Rifle association. The irony, comical pretenses and double standards acts of man, here highlighted because it may be escalating, is aptly depicted by a scene credited to William Gordon: 'What is a political traitor, Daddy?' asked a small boy. 'A man who leaves our party', answered the father; 'and goes over to another'. Then what's a man who leaves another party to come over to ours, Daddy? 'A convert, my boy, a convert'. A fleeting peep, into the slime pit of spin, con and fibbing.

The malaise, like many dreaded diseases has acquired complications. Some of which include, the lavish use of spin and cross reference corroborative excuses from even the animal kingdom. To be more explicit, an example is essential. During the third week of Feb.2013, a number of excited commentaries (especially on the web- www) were made on/about the videoed rare case of a fight of two lions in the East African (Tanzanian) Serengeti. Rare indeed it is and luckily caught on camera. Lions are lower animals. Man, the apex of creation, the developed, the knowledgeable and endowed with comparatively very high brain capacity; so excited about a bout of two big cats in the wild. Some, as if to show that 'we' actually have partners in our shameful violent conducts. That on a daily basis, there is hardly any human well populated ten square kilometers within which an unprovoked squabble, vicious argument, physical violence or killing (murder) does not occur. Also, not just for market places and the like; many gatherings are rather rowdy. That may explain why a few different ones are termed 'solemn assemblies'. Some of those rowdiness transform, on instances into a consuming siege on our periodic need of many moments of tranquility.

Bleak, as most of the facets of the issues seem to remain; but not so for obesity. That years ago, John F Kennedy in admonishing his nation's citizens said: 'we are under-exercised as a nation. We look instead of play. We ride instead of walk. Our existence deprives us of the minimum of physical activity essential for healthy living', is paying-off. The malaise is widely acknowledged. So, in a lot of places (nations), not just eating right and exercise is helping to reduce the severity but food inadequacy apparently does. Allied to that and a show of willingness to be distant from acts of insensitivity; is a FIFA (World Football Governing Body) requirement for the Football (Soccer) World Cup of 2014 in Brazil. By that host nation's World Cup General Bill and Administrative rule No.205, special seats are to be reserved for the obese. That is to meet FIFA's request to accommodate people of disabilities (which include; wheelchair users, obese people and mobility impaired persons).

That said instance of care would bring extended benefits and aid man's self-preservation; if we handle the environment more sustainably to reverse or at least significantly reduce trends that distort the ecosystematic equilibriums. Principally because; current weather and tectonic events are worrisome. Granted that these weather and tectonic phenomenon are known; the issue is that their current frequency, severity, durations and coverage areas seem to have expanded and or shifted from the known (historical records). Thus making it quite difficult, to empathize with the opinions of those who oppose climate change views, in totality. On that, the saying of Patricia Clafford that 'the work will wait while you show the rainbow, but the rainbow won't wait while you do the work' thus ominously resonates. For a sample pick, mention can be made of few natural events of late 2012 to Feb.2013, to support the quest to address the adverse trends:

- As at Sept 9, 2012 very heavy and sustained rainfall induced large scale regional (i.e., from the middle to lower catchment basin of River Niger)

91

flooding in Nigeria. Killed over 137 and displaced 30,000 and inundated some areas for 3-7 weeks.

- Late Sept. (about 24th, 2012) massive sustained rainfall triggered floods and landslides in NE India; caused the death of about 33 and displaced 1,000,000.

- Hurricane Sandy (made landfall in USA on 29th Oct 2012); killed over 130, with record storm surges and floods. Mostly affecting New York and New Jersey coastal areas. Having earlier devastated the Caribbean Islands.

- Typhoon Bopha (by 9th Dec 2012) torrential rains, flash floods and massive mudslides devastated Southern Philippines; with an eventual death toll of over 900.

- On the same day, an off-shore earthquake brought 1meter deep tsunami flood into parts of Japan.

- A wintry high winds storm (on 10th Dec, 2012) blanketed the Mid-Western plains of USA with heavy snowfall. Minneapolis got over 30cm of snow in a short-while.

- On 11th Dec, 2012, a rear 'cluster' of tornadoes slammed the Southern states of USA. Six of such ripped through four states and destroyed homes.

- Jan 25th, 2013, massive rain triggered flooding at Central Mozambique killed 12 persons; while military rescue teams by helicopters rescued 12,000.

- 8th Feb, 2013; a historic winter storm with about 50million persons in its pathway blew across NE USA. The severe 'white-out' caused thousands of schools and flights to be closed/cancelled.

- 10th Feb, 2013: A long lasting incident of solar flare eruption was unleashed by the sun towards the earth. Though not expected to endanger satellites, it could amplify auroras on earth (said the USA, NASA).

- 13th Feb, 2013: After just 5days, a blizzard weary NE, USA had to brace for another snow storm.

- 15th Feb, 2013: A meteorite luckily (ie, without hitting the ground) exploded in Russian sky (in the region of Chelyabinsk). It triggered shockwaves; that caused a factory roof collapse and shattered glass windows thus injuring nearly 1000 persons.

From the entire spate of the reference events, if man has unwittingly and cumulatively or otherwise triggered these reactions or a 'war' with nature, we have less than a half chance of winning even a single side battle. So the situation can be said to be pathetic, foolhardy and deeply naïve; because of the following:

(a)   Our opponent's control of the dynamics is, tight and total.

(b)   Man's knowledge of this abstract opponent remains largely vague.

(c)   Man has; neither the speed, means nor experience, to overwhelm or out-maneuver the opponent; on any of the relatively few battle grounds.

(d)   Man has no effective defense mechanism against the few known opponent's tectonic, meteorological and planetary weapons.

Since we all know the 'opponent' is benevolent and very forgiving, a swift retreat would do. Not an indecisive and sickly diplomatic posturing, like the UN Security Council failure on the Syrian national political situation.

E L Nwankwo   (05/03/2013)

SOURCES

BOOKS: (As referenced within the text)

TABLES: (compiled from records and reports of)
- Reuters.com web news reports
- Encyclopedia Britannica 2010
- Encarta dictionaries 2009

QUOTATIONS:

Encarta dictionaries 2009

Enyi (E L Nwankwo) presentations 1987-2012

Holy Bible (NKJV- New King James Version)

N/B: 1,   COVER PAGE photo peculiar Sept sun-set skyline cloud formation (Port-Harcourt, Nigeria)

2,   BACK PAGE photo (incldg: front page insert) dwindling forested valley system in Umuahia, Nigeria.